THE MESSAGE IN THE STORY

THE MESSAGE IN THE STORY

DISCOVERING AND SHARING THE GOD-GIVEN MESSAGES IN YOUR LIFE

MICA BURNETT

DEDICATION

This book is dedicated first and foremost to my Heavenly Father, who gave me life and carries me through it. By His grace and mercies, I am renewed every day.

To my daughters Lindsey and Laci, who have taught me unconditional love, unfathomable patience, and have inspired me to give my all in everything I do.

To the best girlfriends anyone could ever have, Melena Perdue, for supporting me to finish this book and get it out there. Jana Nabilsi, who has been my spiritual confidante in life's challenges and trials, and Shawn Klein, a forever sister in seeking God's direction. These ladies have played roles in my life that I know were divinely purposed.

I have been blessed with many amazing friendships across my lifetime of which I cherish, and many of them have played parts in the messages I share. I am forever grateful for the light and lessons they have brought into my life. While their names may not be listed here, God knows them intimately.

To Amarillo South Church, Amarillo Texas, Singles group and anonymous members whose support and prayers catapulted my sharing of God' s messages.

Contents

INTRODUCTION

Do you ever wish there were signs and wonders that showed us messages from God today like there were told in the Bible? Do you ever find yourself praying, asking God for a sign or direction? Perhaps you have asked for comfort, assurance, or wisdom. How often do you make the connection of the messages you actually do receive with what you feel the Lord would have for you to know? Are you paying attention?

This book contains various stories of times in my life when I felt very clearly the message I received could have only come from God Himself. No parting of the Red Sea, or fire from Heaven, no loud audible voice and earth-shaking awakening, but messages that so clearly hit home for me, I just knew they came with a purpose and could not be chalked up to coincidence.

Recognizing the messages we're given helps us not only to grow, overcome, flourish, and benefit, but they help us bless others. In fact, they can be the greatest testimony to someone who can relate to your circumstance and is in need of an ever-loving, forgiving God.

It is my desire that these stories stir the remembrance of your own God-given messages and ignite the spark for you to share them. Keep asking for that guidance, direction, blessing, and protection. Yes, and even for those signs. Just be sure to RECEIVE them. Take inventory and see the many you have received. Give thanks for them. And by all means, pass them on!

All my love to you,

Mica Burnett

WHAT ARE YOU TRYING TO SELL ME?

I've worked in somewhat of a marketing or sales aspect for the biggest part of my career. I've witnessed advertising completely evolve with the introduction of social media. Gone are the days of the polished repetitive jingle and flashy commercial that gave you every reason why you simply *must* purchase this new item to keep up with the Joneses. To make you feel so unsatisfied with yourself that you'll eagerly, or even desperately, buy-in to whatever they are selling has been a goal of big business for years.

Today, however, the tables have turned. With the access of live connection within seconds at our fingertips, people want honest genuine recommendations and reviews. The smart consumer will now turn to people they know and trust. They want to hear others' personal experience, especially others who can relate.

Sure, Kim Kardashian might recommend a new hair product or workout pants, and look fabulous while she does it, but I want to hear from that mother of 4, how easy it is to do her hair with a toddler on her hip and if those pants stretch out after a full day of yoga, a daughter's cheer practice, son's soccer game, *and* a PTA fundraiser. Now, that to me, would be an *authentic* endorsement!

Looking at how people are always trying to sell something started me thinking about how we share the Gospel of Christ in this modern age. Are we authentic endorsers or are we trying to "sell something"? Megachurches and prosperity gospel approaches can make some people question the comparison of what is the church, as it is intended by God, and what is big business.

As Christians, we may have no idea how to really approach sharing the message of Christ. Some of us never approach it, because "sales" is just not our bag. We equate sharing the Good News of Jesus with selling vacuums or timeshares, and to be honest, I've been guilty of hearing someone start to "sell me on how I should want to serve Christ" by attending their specific church or joining their denomination, and felt immediately turned off myself.

Perhaps sharing the Good News is just for the Billy Grahams and TD Jakes of the world, the great storytellers and loud evangelists who present the Gospel. Or it's for the missionaries with their exciting stories from far-away places. Surely, we average folks aren't expected to really spread the message, are we?

Perhaps we invite others to church, and just let the preacher take it from there. If the sermon and the music don't lead them, well, at least we got them in the door, eh? But what if they need something more?

Years ago, I memorized copious amounts of scripture so that I could be a better witness when the opportunity arose. Problem was, I wasn't very good at recognizing when the opportunity arrived. I mean, unless someone was facing a terminal illness, or contemplating suicide, I was never sure when to bring up the amazing story of my Jesus. When I did get the chance, I would revert to just sharing what the Bible said, a memorized verse from what I hoped to be most pertinent chapter at the time (that is, if I remembered it correctly). It even felt like a sales script when I approached it that way.

I mean absolutely no offense here, because scripture is " ...God breathed and profitable for teaching, for reproof, for correction, and for training in righteousness." 2 Timothy 3:16. It is one of the most powerful weapons we have. But you see, most of the time, I wasn't in a position of teaching or correcting. I was just being a friend, a shoulder to lean on, or having an ordinary conversation. Funny thing is, I had been publicly speaking for years, but sharing the Gospel, well, that was a different story.

One thing I have learned is that the message of salvation cannot be sold or pitched. It is felt in the heart and really has little to nothing to do with how I choose to "sell" it.

Oh, I've been there, on the receiving end of high pressure more than a few times, and believe me, it wasn't pretty. I was convinced one year at bible camp at the impressionable age of 11 that when I died I would most assuredly go to hell because I had been sprinkled as a baby and not immersed in water for baptism. I was petrified. This was presented around a campfire right before lights out.

I couldn't close my eyes to sleep that night and prodded, complained, and cried (wailed, literally) until the camp counselors were willing to take me down to the river and "properly" baptize me.

It was well after midnight, and with lanterns in hand, it turned into a procession of numerous children who now wanted to get baptized too.

I can't speak for anyone else's heart that night if it was an outpouring of the Holy Spirit or a monkey-see-monkey-do kind of reaction, but I know I was pressured into obedience at that moment.

While honoring and obeying our Father is critical, I find it hard to believe His plan was to send me to the fires of hell if I had somehow died before going under the river current that night. I made that decision in complete fear, and not as a conscious act of honoring or obeying God.

I didn't love Him in a way that I *wanted* to do this for Him. I was saving my own skin from a described torture. It didn't bring me into any close relationship with what He had for me and for my life. In fact, I think it set me up to fear Him in unhealthy and less respectful ways, virtually blocking me from seeing that He was with me and not in some far-away-where-only-perfect-people-may-enter place.

How I viewed God when I was pressured into baptism is just one of many stories.

Every one of us has a story to tell. And not just one. Numerous stories. A life's bounty of experiences. But do we share them?

When was the last time you shared a personal story with someone? We tend to feel safest with our loved ones. Was it a friend or family member? Was the story you shared for a laugh, a memory, or something greater? Were you offering empathy, a minor nugget of wisdom, or an invitation to camaraderie? Stories have ways of offering those things. Yet, not everyone shares their stories.

The world is such a stew of characters, each with their own style and method of gaining and keeping knowledge and insight or sharing it. Some people hold tight to every lesson learned and bury them like treasure. We may never really know how they truly felt about a certain situation or event in their life.

There are times, and there are those people of whom we wonder if they've ever received a message, learned a lesson, or even spent a moment of reflection on their circumstances. Who are we to judge? Ah, but we do!

Most often, we judge ourselves. Just when we think we have a great story to tell, we convince ourselves that it is somehow not good enough. We think we won't be able to express ourselves well.

As a Christian, we are called to share the Good News and be ready to give a reply as to why we accept Jesus Christ as our Savior. The Apostle Peter tells us in 1 Peter 3:15 to "... **Always be prepared to give an answer to everyone who asks you to give the reason for the hope that you have."**

Over the years, I have seen the example of very popular evangelists and speakers and thought to myself, "What charisma it must take to share the really big life changing stories!" But see, I didn't consider that it is more often the little stories that make the biggest impact in our lives.

The little relatable stories.

We tend to think that God is so far away and out of our physical reach, but He has shown Himself to be so much closer. He is in our every day. I believe He sends messages throughout creation. Signs in nature, flashes of memory or intuition, visual cues, and conversations, the kindness of strangers, and intentional personal sacrifices.

If we purposely take a moment to open our eyes and focus our hearts, we will see Him in our average ordinary day. Not the spotlight, the drama trauma, the edge of life experience, though He can be in all those things too. I believe there can be great epiphanies in the mediocre life. I know there has been for mine.

I am no one special. In fact, I fail on a regular basis in many aspects of life. If you were to judge me by the world's standards, I am nothing to look at or follow. Yet there are messages in my story that are not meant to be kept quiet. The messages are not only for me. God's scripture holds the ultimate power, but there is a unique script that was written just for me. And by simply sharing my story I am sharing what a difference Christ has made for me.

I hope my stories encourage you to dig into yours and recognize the power that is in the simple recollection and sharing of them. There is a message in them, in every one of them, if you really want to find it.

There is a healing, a kinship, and a hand that can guide another heart to seeing God in their life too, simply because they could relate to what you shared with them.

No fancy words. No memorized speech. No verbatim "Scriptural Scholar" skills are needed. Just tell people your own personal story of how God has worked in your life, in a moment, or what He has shown you in any given circumstance. God will lead them to a deeper knowledge when they get hungry and seek Him. You are simply sharing a piece of your cake.

God, in a mediocre life? Yes, my friend, yes! He is in the icing, and the gooey middle layers, and the cherry on top, but better still, His works are stirred right up in the batter! Psalm 34:8 says "Taste and see that the Lord is good; blessed is the one who takes refuge in Him."

I love sweets, and I have found my God and His mercies to be the sweetest of all.

Shall we dig in?

REFLECTION JOURNAL : WHAT ARE YOU TRYING TO SELL ME?

Each chapter will be followed by a reflection journal. This is a time for you alone or with a study partner or group, to reflect upon your feelings and personal stories related to the chapter topic. Feel free to copy and distribute these pages for completion.

How to approach discussing Christianity can be as unique and multi-faceted as your own personality. Most of us have our own opinions based on what we have experienced personally. Let's think about that for a moment.

Think of a time you were invited to church, someone

discussed their religious beliefs with you or shared their reasons for accepting Christ. Describe it briefly here:

What felt good about it? Why? Or Why not?

What turned you off by it? Why or Why Not?

Have you ever shared your testimony with another person?

Is it easy for you to share your testimony? Why or Why not?

Are you comfortable sharing personal stories and memories with others? Why or why not?

Would finding the message of God's blessing, intervention, lesson, connection, or provision be helpful in sharing your stories, and enhance your testimony?

THERE IS A MESSAGE IN THE STORY OF YOUR RELATIONSHIP WITH GOD.

THE OLD BAIT AND SWITCH

There was a time in my life where the culmination of events was just too much to bear. It's enough to complete an entire book itself and perhaps one day will. For now, let's suffice it to say that I couldn't imagine a loving God being anywhere close to me. If He did exist, He was for other people. You know, the ones with the intact families, who ate dinner together at the table every evening and dressed up for church on Sundays.

God didn't live in broken homes with innocence lost and drunken screams. If He did, surely, He would have stepped in to protect me, I thought. I must be something atrocious, for my father to leave and never come back. For my mother to so blatantly hate me. For my stepfather to abuse me.

I desperately sought love in immature places, resulting in

pregnancy at fourteen and its proceeding abortion against my will. I won't go into that story here, but its events led me to become a walking death wish.

I tried overdosing once by consuming a family-sized bottle of aspirin. It was the only type of "drug" I had access to at the time. Surely a whole bottle would do the trick, I thought. As my stomach began aching, I went to the nurse's office at school and asked her, "Hypothetically, if a person was to commit suicide with aspirin, how would they die exactly? I'm just curious."

"Well, unfortunately, it would be rather grim," she said. "I imagine because aspirin is pretty acidic, it would tear up the stomach lining, causing internal bleeding. The person would probably die by choking as they vomited their own blood." Just then, a huge abdominal cramp doubled me over and it became obvious that I needed medical help.

Of course, my mother was called to accompany me to the emergency room. I remember her disappointment in me as the words spit through her teeth. If I was going to kill myself, I should have at least done it right and foregone the unnecessary embarrassment of involving schools and hospitals.

I was a failure in the purest sense, unable to even check myself out correctly. So, what was the point of living? To just wait for the inevitable day of death? What a drudgery of joylessness. Emptiness. Nothingness. I felt that hell was all that awaited me and yet to live was hell itself.

I went through the next few years living from one extreme to the next. Either completely numb and dead to life or climbing the nearest success ladder to prove myself. Although I married, it was all a show. I didn't love myself. In fact, I loathed myself.

How could I possibly share in love with another human being? I looked to my husband for some validation that I was still human, still somehow lovable. He had no idea the depth of my sorrow or inner reflection. We were married in a nightclub, it was an extraordinary party, with everyone invited, except Christ. The majority of our wedding blessings were given as drunken cheers! Woohoo! (Spoken softly with a very sad bit of sarcasm)

We were charged an extra fee to have the Justice of the Peace perform our wedding in the nightclub, where of course, no member of the clergy was willing to officiate the ceremony. Red flag? I was color blind. Red looked green to me. At least I was married now. That was better than being alone, wasn't it? Poor, little, confused girl. She didn't know.

It wasn't until numerous failed relationships later, living in my car behind the library, and every failed attempt to be good enough, did my life make a serious turn.

I was in my second marriage. Another unhealthy coupling, and one in which I did everything to appear perfect to the world. We had a successful business. I taught Sunday School and was an AWANA leader at church. I was the first to show up at church and the last to leave. The one who baked herself silly for every funeral, wedding, or invited event. The one who never said "No". I was Joyce Meyer's supreme definition of Suzy Super Christian.

Maybe if I could just stretch myself far enough, God could forgive me. Maybe He would come closer to me, maybe not save me because I didn't deserve that, I thought, but perhaps I could find a little bit of His mercy.

I worked so hard at perfection I was exhausted and resentful most days, but plodded on. Praying for others and praising the good and the grace God bestowed on them while feeling empty and disconnected inside.

Music was a constant companion for me. It has always been a passion of mine and whenever I felt down or lonely, I would sing. I have been singing as long as I can remember. It's all about the lyrics for me. Words have a way of coming alive. I have journals of poetry from my early adolescence where I had poured out my soul onto every page. A page doesn't judge you or feel sorry for you. It just soaks it all in.

So, back to my second marriage. I was at a thrift store looking through cassette tapes. There was a box of about 15 new tapes, unopened and still in plastic that was selling for 50 cents. The entire box! I knew this was a steal, but I didn't recognize a single artist in the group. Names like Jars of Clay, Steven Curtis Chapman, Crystal Lewis, and Rich Mullins were all Greek to me. Certainly no one famous, I thought. But for half a dollar, surely there must be at least one good song or two, so I took them home and began listening.

There was a cassette by Kathy Troccoli called Love and Mercy, and I remember having it play randomly in the car. As I was driving, a song came on about a baby in Heaven asking God to forgive the mother that aborted him. I had to pull the car over and weep uncontrollably. No one, I mean no one, in my world would ever talk about the abortion, and here someone was singing it? Acknowledging it still as a tragedy, yet one in which forgiveness can still be had. I was in awe that this was not only in words but in song.

Another song of Kathy's simply repeated, "Help me, God, I'm scared and I'm unprepared to face the night alone." I found myself tearfully wailing along with the words, "Heal me. Hear my prayer. My soul, it aches and I've nowhere to go. In this dark hour, I know only the Power that made the stars can mend my heart."

Though married, so isolated in my shame and pain was I that I might as well have been in solitary confinement. How could this woman understand exactly what I was feeling? I literally played that tape until the ribbon wore off and had to purchase a new one!

I would call my best friend or gather my husband to listen.

"Listen to the words!" I would excitedly say, but they would just drift off in conversation, not getting what I was experiencing. I know now that is because that experience was just for me.

You see every song, every lyric, every verse that poured into my soul was a breath that had been timed just for me. Whenever I played them, I was in prayer, and in worship, whether I realized it or not. I was releasing and surrendering years of pain, and guilt and shame. I was crying out to Him the things I had kept so long inside.

God was using exactly what He knew would reach me. There was no person who could have sold me on God's forgiveness. I was content to walk in my numbness and accept my feeling that God was not for me. But then He spoke to my heart in song.

The old Bait and Switch. Pull me in with what interests me one minute and then have me fully snot-faced and flung out on the floor in surrender the next. Pretty genius. But then again, He's God and He'll use whatever means necessary for us to get the message.

Has God shown up in a way that truly hit home for you? Has He used something that is close to your heart, a hobby, a connection or even a relationship where you can see there was a message that was obviously just for you?

Sometimes the message is glaringly apparent and can come about as loud as a slap in the face. Other times, it may take awhile to sink in or it must grow and bear fruit before we can look back and see where the message first began.

Don't give up on seeking His messages. God says, "You will seek me and find me when you seek me with all your heart." Jeremiah 29:13

The viewpoint from which we reflect on our life's events has a way of changing over time. Just like getting new revelations when reading scripture we have read even many times before, there is the opportunity to see new messages that were hidden when we previously recalled a memory.

Let your memories be the bait and see what message your focus will be switched to when you seek what God has for you to know.

REFLECTION JOURNAL: THE OLD BAIT AND SWITCH

Some of the most meaningful experiences can come when the Holy Spirit uses what is most familiar to us to get our attention. Usually, it is a time when we are focused on something that really speaks to us on a deeply personal level.

Perhaps in music or written words. Often in art forms, such as painting or sculpting. Creating. Isn't that amazing? We have the ability to create something, build something from scratch. Repair what is broken, mend what is coming apart. Are you noticing any similarities here?

It is usually in our hobbies and special interests, that we find ourselves so focused we experience what is known as "flow".

It is a feeling of being fully immersed and involved in an activity. Some call it being "in the zone."

Spending time in nature can elicit similar feelings when one is able to detach from all other distractions and worries, and just experience the moment. Music has always done that for me. I can get completely lost in the words of a song or beautiful melody and find myself weeping uncontrollably. Not sad, by any means. The tears just start flowing as if they are crying out praises to God.

I used to hide the tears because they were difficult to explain and someone nearby would always try to comfort and console me, thinking I was sad. On the contrary, it was a feeling of experiencing God's grace and mercies that was so beautiful, so amazing, it can only be felt.

I knew a woman who experienced something similar. When she really connected to Praise music she started dancing and raising her hands. She too, felt embarrassed, as some people stared, or even ridiculed her.

She told me the feeling was so overwhelmingly joyous that she finally got to the point of no longer resisting it. "Why would I refuse the most energizing fuel up for the week because someone else wants to call me strange?" She told me.

I couldn't help but grin from ear to ear every time I saw her "worship dancing" at church. It was her boldness and open joy that moved some people to come forward and accept Christ, and to think, she could have chosen to keep it in!

Have you ever felt God's presence when you were immersed in an activity, publicly or privately?

How did it feel while it was happening? Did you go with it, or shut it down?

How did it feel afterward?

Have you experienced it since then?

Have you ever shared that with anyone?

THERE IS A MESSAGE IN THE STORY OF HOW GOD CONNECTED WITH YOU.

GROWING IN HARD GROUND

There are a million reasons I can offer regarding why I was not successful in not one but two marriages. We could debate until the cows come home on how God feels about divorce, what the Bible says, what religion says, and what any other outsider looking in can say about the collapse of my relationships, but there's not enough room for that here.

I can't imagine a relationship any more broken than my marriage when I first decided to dig a pond. I just needed something to occupy my time and my mind and some physical exertion seemed appropriate. It would be a healthy outlet for me and besides, we lived on the outskirts of Amarillo, Texas. Any added water would be a plus!

It was a dry and barren red-clay desert with nary a tree or tumbleweed. With the sound of the wind and the sheer look of desolation for as far as the eye could see, I felt a pond would be a great transformation, both literally and metaphorically.

I spent days digging and digging that unforgiving ground. When it just wouldn't give, I flooded it and proceeded to dig out the mud pit I had made. It seemed to go a bit faster. It was almost summertime and the temperatures were a dry 90-degree heat, so I would go out as early in the morning as possible to do my dirty work.

I've never been one to read or follow directions, and so decided I would figure it out as I go along, not really knowing what my finished product might be. Perhaps there is a lesson in that as well. But at the time, I didn't see any lessons. I knew only struggles. Struggles in communicating. Struggles in understanding. Struggles with feeling loved.

Every time a tumbleweed blew into me, I would think, "Yep, that's about right, a thousand miles of flat open land, and you run SMACK into me!"

At last, the hole was deep enough for my liking and I lined it with a black tarp, held down by a few choice rocks I had collected. It was time to fill the pond. Luckily, I had dug the hole just a few short feet from the front entrance to our home. That was where the most shade was when there was any. I would soon be able to sit on my porch bench and enjoy the water scenery.

The hose was long enough to reach so I didn't figure I

would need any kind of filter or hose system for the pond. I thought that may be costly anyway in this Texas heat, with the water evaporating so quickly, I figured I can just add it myself when the urge hit me. I topped off the pond, shut off the hose, and stared proudly at my new creation. I had completed it all on my own!

I sat awhile on the bench, admiring my hard work. It still needed a few simple touches. Since flowers didn't take too kindly to the local terrain, I added some potted artificial bouquets to add a touch of color, a few knick-knacky type garden statues and called it a day.

Later that evening, I was awakened by the dogs barking and went for a look outside. I opened the door only briefly when I noticed the metropolis of life around the new pond.

Numerous toads had appeared, from where, I wondered, as they were not normally seen in the area. Attracted to these fine toads, of course, were snakes. As I watched two long snakes slither across my front entry, I abruptly shut the door!

Perhaps having this pond so close to the house was not such a good idea. Maybe a pond that was not much more than a lined hole in the ground wasn't a great idea either. I am sure the nocturnal gang that had arrived at this new hangout would beg to differ, but I didn't create quite the oasis I expected. I wanted a pond, not a snake pit. Needless to say, it wasn't long before this creepy crawly pest attractant was refilled with dirt and I was back to square one in making some kind of aesthetic improvement to the desert that was my front yard.

This time, I set my sights on beautifying the landscape by planting trees. My mother offered to help in the endeavor because as I said, the ground here was truly not conducive to growth outside of the occasional cactus or aloe vera plant. After a trip to Lowes and some advice on trees that were indigenous to the area, we set out to dig eight holes and get to planting.

We were relentless in watering every day and praying that the local crosswinds would be merciful enough to give these little guys a chance. It was a common joke, and very much truth, that you knew you were in the Texas Panhandle because all the trees faced North. The winds grew them that way. The Panhandle gusts were harsh, but even as the water splashed back upon me in the wind, I would faithfully water every morning and evening.

Nothing. Not a change. Not a sprout. Not a sign of life in months. I kept praying for them. I added Miracle Grow tree food. Nothing. No change. Again, I frustratingly decided this was just another symbolism for my life.

My empty marriage. Dead branches with no growth, no matter what I pour into it.

No matter the sweat, the tears, the prayers, the new and greatest efforts, it was out of my control. There was no magical spell and I found myself powerless. Even trying to dress up the environment did not work to cover the desolate fascade and the empty rooms inside my house.

I eventually gave up. Not just on ponds and trees, but on my marriage. After counseling in both church and professional settings, and countless sleepless nights, I decided to cry, "uncle!" To admit defeat and walk away was an utterly soul-wrenching decision that came as a last and final resort.

I remember waiting. Hoping. Looking behind me for my husband to show up and say this was all a big mistake and we'd get through it together. But over time more and more confirmations would arrive to let me know the finality of what was gone.

Before the divorce was official, my father shared his heart with me and told me, in whatever we do, we all will face God one day to explain ourselves, so we should always ask, "Did I do everything I could possibly do?" If the answer is truly and sincerely yes, we can only leave things in God's hands from there.

Feeling the guilt of knowing I couldn't answer "yes" just yet, I called my soon to be ex-husband and told him that when I entered the covenant of marriage with him, I truly meant it. "We don't have to take this road to divorce." He angrily replied that he was NEVER going back. I agreed that I had no interest in going back to how we lived either, and that was why I had to leave, but if he wanted to move forward together, take a new road, I was willing to commit to that as his wife.

I held my breath. I knew that if he said yes, neither of us were healthy enough to make it, that the only way we had a chance was to surrender everything to God and let him handle it. Surrendering to God was not one of our strengths at the time, and certainly not one of strong and independent me, I'll admit. Inwardly I whispered, "Not my will but yours, Lord. Help me accept that." Then came my husband's response, "No. We're done. I'll see you in court!"

What word can describe the feeling of relief and utter sadness at the same time? There is none. There was nothing more I could do than to get out of God's way and see what He had next in store for me on this journey of life.

A few months went by before it came time to drive out to the house in the country and pick up the items divided among us in the divorce. There was a new woman living there with my now ex-husband. As my dog ran out to greet me, she quickly called him off and back inside. I took a good look around, something was different and it wasn't even her being there.

There were trees! Tall, lean trees, about 6 to 8 feet in height, full of green leaves, swaying in the breeze and of course, proudly leaning North! They lined the entire fence!

In my astonishment, I went over to one and just stood

there touching the leaves and praising God. I heard the woman say, "What is she doing over there at the tree?" I must have appeared crazy, adoring the trees like that. I just grinned from ear to ear.

I had surrendered, see. I let go. I kept trying so hard to bring life, to fix, to control, to manipulate that which when finally released, became free. This new life was God telling me, loud and clear, that now the choking earth is gone and His hand will be my nourishment. That even out of miry clay, there is a reaching for the sky.

I suddenly understood, now in this unplanned and awkward moment, that in letting go and getting myself out of the way, God could finally do His work in my life. Provide the growth and healing that I needed. I prayed that symbol was meant for both of us, me and my ex. A new beginning.

Isn't that odd? You'd think I would have resented the fact that once I left, the trees sprung to life. But that was the irony of the message, you see. I knew in the instant I saw those trees that God had lined that driveway just for me in luscious green. His message rang loud and clear to my heart.

"And all the trees in the field shall know that I am the Lord; I bring low the high tree and make high the low tree, dry up the green tree, and make the dry tree flourish. I am the Lord; I have spoken, and I will do it." Ezekial 17:24 (ESV)

God assured me even in this new unclear path, He is Lord. It's all His, ya know. Trees. Marriages. Everything. I've learned the sooner I release control, the better growth. In trees, in me, in everything.

REFLECTION JOURNAL: GROWING IN HARD GROUND

We have probably all heard, countless times, that whenever God closes one door He opens another. Or maybe it's a window. I'm not sure who originally quoted that, or if it matters whether it's a door or window, the point is that there is an opening. A place for the light to come in and shine on what was once dark. An opening for a fresh burst of air where perhaps before we struggled to breathe. A new journey, a new opportunity is waiting for us when we recognize this.

Think of a time you found yourself at the end of something. Perhaps you didn't realize it was the end. It felt like a brick wall. A dead end. A challenge that no matter how hard you tried, things did not seem to go in your favor.

What was it?

What happened that made the situation change?

Were you asking for God's help or blessing? (Even if the answer was not what you asked for?)

Did you recognize God's hand in changing the circumstance? At the time? Or did you recognize this later?

How did you feel after the situation changed? Free? Released from burden? Excited? Grateful?

How hard has it been to trust God over the direction of your life?

THERE IS A MESSAGE IN THE STORY OF YOUR FOLLOWING A NEW DIRECTION.

HOLDING IT ALL TOGETHER

I had an old GMC Safari. It had well close to 200 thousand miles on the engine when I purchased it with all I had at the time, which let me tell you, wasn't very much. It was the first vehicle I could muster together after starting over again from another broken marriage. I was proud to have a vehicle. It meant I was one step closer to an easier life for us. A way to school, a means for emergencies. The freedom of not having to ask for rides or staying confined to the women's shelter where my two girls and I lived temporarily trying to lay out the path for a new life.

It wasn't too long after I bought it that the little maroon van began smoking. It drank oil like a skid row alcoholic guzzles cold medicine. I did my best to keep up with topping it off daily and parking in areas that it didn't completely ruin the landscape with pools of oil. I became accustomed to this process as just a norm of being able to drive. But something new started happening. I could feel it when the car got up in speed. It was a shaking, a wobbling, that once we were on the highway at a constant high speed, it seemed to stop.

With no money for a mechanic, my girls and I would pray every day before we got into the van that the Good Lord would keep us safe while I tried to figure out a means for another vehicle.

My income tax refund came in and with that, the hope of trading the van and getting something with fewer problems was on the horizon. I remember the first car lot I visited was all ready to trade, the only thing left was their inspection of my vehicle. I gave them the keys and waited for their offer.

A very troubled looking young manager came back to ask me, "Mam do you happen to have any other vehicle?" I said, "No, that's why I am here, why?" "Well, I'm afraid we're unable to do a trade today. You see, there is only one bolt on the motor mount holding your engine up. Seems all the others have somehow broken off. It needs quite a bit of work. So much in fact that I can't let you drive it home. It's just not safe."

Against better judgment, I did what many desperate people in my situation might do. I waited for the right moment to get my keys from the service desk while the manager was busy talking with another customer and speedily drove away. What was I to do, with no other vehicle, little money, and two children depending on me?

I prayed. Hard.

I reminded God of His promises. I can't imagine how many times He has heard me nagging like a downtrodden wife needing the trash taken out again, but He was my only hope.

A short time after, I was driving downtown, yes, in the same van with one bolt holding it together and passed a car lot with a little white Pontiac convertible sitting out front.

For some reason it's presence pulled me in and I decided to stop and take it for a test drive. I'd always wanted a convertible and to be honest I thought it was silly of me to be test driving this when I could not afford it and didn't have any value in my van for a decent trade.

Convincing myself that a good fantasy should be given a test drive every once in a while, just to keep our dreams alive, I took her for a spin.

The car dealer told me that the little sports coup had a salvaged title and so he couldn't ask for full value but he assured me that it was mechanically sound. He said he would be willing to do a straight across title trade. Nervously, I asked if he wanted to take my van for a full inspection before committing to a deal. I'll never forget what he said. "I was just sitting here asking the Lord who I could help today, and you drove in, so I think we're good" and he walked right into his office to start the paperwork!

I felt a little guilty as I drove away in my new, little, used convertible. After all, I couldn't force him to inspect the van, and I did suggest it a couple of times. Who am I to question someone's obedience? The irony is this, I didn't really appreciate that God had a hand in this, I really felt I was getting away with something, so even though it felt good, it felt just a little bit wrong.

I loved that little convertible. My girls and I drove around town as if we were in a parade, with people waving when we passed. We practiced our best pageant waves and felt like royalty.

A couple of weeks had passed when the dealer called and asked me to come in to pick up my new tags. When I arrived, he met me in the lot with a huge smile. He said, "The funniest thing happened the other day." I held my breath. "Here it comes, I'm busted," I thought. "We took that van to the auto auction and as soon as it was on display, they started her up, and you'll never believe this," He laughed. "The motor just fell out! Had a bad motor mount, craziest thing you've ever seen!"

I hung my head expecting now to have to give the car back. The jig was up. "Isn't that amazing," he said, "How God answers prayer? Good thing you got out of that van before that happened to you and your girls on a highway!"

That little Sunfire carried me all the way through nursing school, and to this day reminds me that when you are barely hanging on, God still has a plan that is holding it all together.

In **Deuteronomy 31:8** the Bible says "The Lord is the one who goes ahead of you; He will be with you. He will not fail you or forsake you. Do not fear or be dismayed."

Looking back, I can see how we were safely carried in that dangerous accident-waiting-to-happen until landing right near the one who could help. And not just that that car dealer could, but that he purposely chose to as he felt led to do!

Our daily praying over that van wasn't a silly practice in faith. I believe it was an authoritative act set in motion by us being willing to say it. Even then, all the while I lived in survival mode, God was working things out for me and my family. Sometimes I ask the Holy Spirit to increase my faith, because as a human some things I struggle to see, like the light at the end of the tunnel. But I do know Who is the light and if I just acknowledge that it gets me out of the way of His best plans for me.

"For I know the plans I have for you," declares the Lord, "plans to prosper you and not to harm you, plans to give you a hope and a future." Jeremiah 29:11

REFLECTION JOURNAL: HOLDING IT ALL TOGETHER

Looking back over your life, have there been any circumstances of which you now find yourself saying, "I don't know how I ever made it through that!" Times, that make you think there's really no way you could have survived that on your own? The older I get, the more of those I realize I have had!

Life is so full of hardships, from death to divorce, disease to addiction, poverty to abuse. Yet somehow, somewhere we might experience a moment of relief, a helping hand up, a shoulder to lean on, a blessing in disguise.

Sometimes a family member, friend, or even total stranger appears just at the right time. Something happens out of the blue. We see a message, perhaps even no one else sees, but it changes everything.

What have you experienced that could have taken a different turn but somehow didn't? You survived, You changed, you went a different direction.

Why do you think things changed for you?

Was there any person or particular message involved in the change?

Did you ask God to help you in this situation or discover that He was intervening for you? At the time, or in looking back?

Have you shared this story with anyone?

47

THERE IS A MESSAGE IN THE STORY OF YOUR SURVIVING OR OVERCOMING A HARDSHIP.

TACO TESTIMONY

Lindsey hurried in from school and rushed to put her books down. "Mama! Mama! I have a surprise to show you!" She opened her backpack and carefully pulled out a small certificate that recognized her for good citizenship at school.

This child of mine was always being recognized for her caring heart and good example. She prided herself on buddying-up to every stray animal, the new kid at school, or the cause that no one else would volunteer for. She worked hard for any penny she earned and rarely ever just asked for anything outright without first offering to wash the car, rake the yard, or help with various tasks.

Beaming with a bit of pride myself, and grateful that it was close to suppertime I noticed the certificate entitled her to a free meal at a local taco joint. "Why don't we go collect on this right now?" I said. "Oh really? Mama, that would be awesome!" So, we loaded ourselves into the car and headed for a little taco treat.

We decided to get our meal "to go" so we could get home and watch some videos we had checked out from the library. As we were pulling from the drive-thru lane, my daughter asked me to circle back around. I wondered why. "Did we forget something?" "Please Mama, just drive back around the building one more time." So, I did. And there he was.

A man in old dirty clothes, with matted hair and filthy hands, was digging through the dumpster for scraps. Rolling down the window, Lindsey yelled, "Sir! Sir!" and he looked up before slowly approaching us. Oh boy, I thought, here he comes straight to my daughter's side window. What if he's not mentally stable, or even dangerous? But he was already to the car, window all the way down, and my little girl smiling from ear to ear.

"I won this meal today at school and I just wanted you to have it, "she beamed, as she passed her prize through the open window. He took the bag and its warm aromatic contents, smiling shyly and said, "Thanks." He rushed away to go behind the dumpsters to eat.

I shared with my daughter how amazed I was with her generosity and we said a prayer for him together, Then I turned the car to head back through the drive-thru to order her another meal for supper. "No thanks, Mama, I don't need anything else," she declared matter-of-factly, although she still hadn't eaten. "I'm really kind of full," she said as she leaned back in her seat smiling.

Yes, my darling you are full, so very full of light and love and hope, and I have been privileged to witness the testimony that is you.

"Do not forget to show your hospitality to strangers, for by so doing some people have shown hospitality to angels without knowing it." Hebrews 13:2 (NIV)

REFLECTION JOURNAL: TACO TESTIMONY

Have you ever witnessed a selfless act of another person? Some people seem to be full of them, almost as a way of life. While others feel moved in just the right opportunity or special moment to step up and help someone. Volunteers who expect nothing in return, no notoriety or acknowledgment, yet feel rewarded by doing what they felt compelled to do are some of my favorite people.

Think of a time you may have witnessed someone helping another in brotherly love that made an impression on you. What was it and why did this impress you?

Has watching someone else help others ever caused you to consider helping or getting involved in some way?

Have you ever witnessed the kind acts of others (or service you have offered yourself) change someone's day, moment, or even life?

List any volunteer work you have been involved in or would consider.

Ever done anything secretly to help or bless someone? Why or Why not? If so, how did it make you feel afterward?

Have you ever been blessed by someone's help, donation, an act of service, or even a secret gift? If so, how did it make you feel?

55

Has seeing someone else's act of service to another or being on the receiving end of it, caused you to thank or even praise God?

THERE IS A MESSAGE IN YOUR STORY OF SERVICE.

HAPPY MEALS AND DIVINE INTERSECTIONS

It was midsummer in the late 90s, and in the Texas panhandle, that meant for a hot, dry afternoon. I was a single mother of 2 girls, 5 and 11. Recently divorced and doing everything I could to rub two nickels together to stay afloat. We lived in assisted housing. You know, the kind that charges next to nothing for rent if you agree to attend college and maintain a healthy grade point average. It was a hand up, and one I appreciated greatly.

The girls came in from the playground panting and searching to relieve their thirst. After guzzling a good half gallon of water, they turn to me with the most darling manipulative grins. "You know what sounds so good now, Mama?" Dare I ask? They would tell me anyway. "A pop!

A great big icy cold soda! Can we get one? Please? Please? Please?"

There was a corner store a short drive away that sold fountain drinks for only 37 cents. Big styrofoam cups filled with 44 ounces of chemical sweetness that were large enough to share. All we needed was to gather 37 measly cents. I informed the girls of our mission, and we proceeded to dig under every couch cushion, in every coat pocket, old purse, and car seat until we had found, yes, *exactly* one quarter, one dime, and two shiny pennies!

Excitedly to the store we went. So accomplished I felt in this small task because you see, life was hard back then. It was a struggle daily to get by. I entered every scholarship competition I could get into for extra cash while in school. I worked part-time and was in nursing school, away from the girls from 5 am each morning until after 7 each evening. Then studying all night.

We were all in counseling due to the scars of domestic violence. The determination to show my children that its nasty cycle stopped with us was what kept me going even when it was difficult. We lived on faith and caseloads of Ramen noodles, so the sweet wet treat of a cold soda on a summer day sounded as delicious as a day at the spa.

Pulling into the parking lot of our apartment, with our new bucket-o-cola, I noticed the girls had gotten oddly quiet. It was common to hear them bicker, "Mom! She's taking too long a sip! Mom, it's my turn, she's gonna drink it all!" But this time, all I heard was sniffling. I looked back in the mirror to see my five-year-old, Laci, shoulders slumped defeatedly, staring at me.

"Mama?" she said in the most innocent trembling voice. "Yes, baby, what's wrong?" I asked. "Do you think maybe one day God will let me have my own pop?" She wasn't asking in a selfish or demanding way. She sincerely found herself contemplating the fact that nothing was sacred in our family.

We were living in a way that everything had to be shared, at least for a time. While that's not such a bad thing in and of itself, the fact that she was feeling God didn't offer something just for her made her feel less loved.

Now usually, I have a gift for words. I can find the right outlook and tweak it just enough to instill hope and come across sounding like some wise sage, but this day was not the day. My stress level was wound beyond extremely tight and my emotions were raw due to a million things including, I am sure, that roller coaster hormonal time of the month when vocal filters seem to be in short supply. I lost my cool.

Right there, in front of my children, I sat in the van, banging on the steering wheel, and barking at God like a junkyard dog. "You PROMISED you are the father to the fatherless, the husband to the widow, Jehovah Jireh our

PROVIDER, God, and I can't even gather more than 37 cents for my kids! I can't do anymore! You PROMISED if we seek you first that everything else is added, well, where is it? I am struggling to see it, Lord!!"

I was in the extreme throws of my temper tantrum when I heard a tapping on the driver side window. I slowly turned my head to the left. There stood a woman I had never seen before, standing back just far enough that she seemed afraid.

"Great!" I thought, "she must think I am abusing my children! Wonderful!" I barely rolled the window down a crack to tell her everything was fine, when she quickly said, "Please don't think I'm weird, I just had a really strong feeling that God was telling me I needed to give you this." She slipped a twenty-dollar bill in through the opening and then left so abruptly, I didn't even get a chance to thank her.

The girls seemed to be experiencing the same feeling I was, as we all sat in complete silence for a few moments. Then I began crying, humbly thanking God for this kind act of a stranger. I apologized for my tone and how I yelled at Him. Then too, I encouraged my girls to never stop reminding God of His promises. I think He likes to know that we rely on them and still trust in Him regardless of our circumstance., and even in our emotional human frailties.

Does God care about something as little as a 37 cent

pop? Sweet friend, it is so much deeper than that, but yes, if that is how He can touch you, then yes, yes, He does!

We drove to McDonald's then and for the first time in a very long time, we were all treated to our very own "happy meal" and I do mean happy!

When was the last time you felt God calling you to do something? Did you listen? You may never know how your simple act of obedience may play a part in a person's greater healing. I just know those blessings come full circle.

A prime example of that is this. Months later, there was a terrible thunderstorm with flash flooding. I heard pounding on my door in the late evening and was afraid to open it. We didn't live in the greatest neighborhood and it was after dark. I somehow felt led to open the door anyway. There standing drenched in the pounding rain was a woman and her three children.

"Please, can you just make a call for me?" she pleaded, "I can't get anyone to help and I need the landlord, our keys washed away in the flood and we are locked out of both my apartment and car!" I motioned them all in, helped them get dry and contacted the landlord. It was a little while before any help could arrive and I offered them to stay the night. I couldn't shake the feeling that I knew her from somewhere. She seemed oddly familiar.

Later in our conversation, she mentioned something about trying to be faithful to listen when God tells her to do something. She recently came into a small inheritance and for some reason, she felt God kept moving her to bless other people. This was a struggling single mother herself, mind you, just following that pull on her heart.

It was then that her face flashed across my mind, passing me that twenty through the van window! She lived in the same complex, just on the very end. We had parked on opposite sides of the building and our paths never crossed until they were divinely purposed.

Call it what you will. Karma. Chance. Coincidence. A cool cosmic accident. I choose to believe it was by divine design. You see, that precious woman became a dear friend to me, and is to this day. We have prayed for each other, been there for each other through marriages, and celebrations, to deaths, and loss, and daily strife. Tears of joy and tears of laughter, lifelong sisters are we. All because we chose to listen when we felt led.

Times of need are opportunities to be a light. Times when strangers are meant to be the friends bearing blessings and aid. "When I was hungry you gave me something to eat. I was thirsty, and you gave me something to drink, I was a stranger, and you invited me in..." Jesus Christ explains in a parable in Matt 25:35, and to that, the King replied, "Truly I tell you, whatever you did for one of the least of these brothers and sisters of mine, you did for me." Matt. 25:40.

May we all walk with our eyes open and listen with a heart prepared to act when the time comes.

REFLECTION JOURNAL: HAPPY MEALS AND DIVINE INTERSECTIONS

Have you ever crossed paths with someone you just know was brought into your life on purpose? Who was it and why do you feel it was meant to be?

Ever met a stranger and felt an immediate connection or kindred spirit? One that you can't explain?

I posted on Facebook my experience with a person like that.

There is a soul I recognize every time I see her, which is only twice a year briefly during a work event. Though I do not know her personally, we are related in spirit. We met over lunch a few years back and immediately started praying over each other. Odd you might think, with someone you just met, but it was the most natural thing. It was like we had known each other forever. Ever since, every Spring and Fall I would seek her out to connect for a brief moment that is more powerful than most months of my year. Tears flow unashamedly as we share scripture and encouragement. People see the tears and ask whats wrong but its whats so amazingly right!! I don't have to understand God's ways because I simply can't but I am so grateful for the comfort and the filling He provides. It's so powerful. I love my job and I am blessed to do what I do. I work with some amazing people who pray with me and for me. We can always find things to complain about regrading our jobs or our lives, but today I was blessed to be at work when God once again sent that kindred spirit to feed my soul. As long as I have breath I will sing praises to my God. He is good ALL the time!

Has the Lord ever met a need for you in an unconventional way? If so, how?

Have you found yourself crying out to God, angry or confused at your situation? What was the reason?

How did you feel afterward?

Why do you think that is?

THERE IS A MESSAGE IN THE STORY OF YOUR DIVINE ENCOUNTERS.

ARE YOU READY FOR A MIRACLE?

Some guys have all the luck. And by that, I mean the worst of luck. My heart sank as I stared across the atrium and saw him, shoulders slumped over, head down with his chin almost dragging the floor, sitting next to her while she was sobbing. He looked up and our eyes met.

He immediately stood up and was headed straight for me with a determined look on his face. "Are you the hotel's restaurant manager?" "Yes, sir, how can I help you?" "Whew, thank God! We're having the worst trip of our lives but nothing a little champagne won't fix. I need a bottle of champagne now please." "Sir, it's Sunday and due to the liquor law, I am unable to provide any alcohol until after noon today."

"No! That's not good enough!" He pleaded, "You don't

understand! I was supposed to propose this weekend. We were going on a tropical vacation, everything was perfect until we missed our flight. The next one was supposed to connect here but our luggage never arrived! We missed our check-in and were stranded for hours, now the weekend is almost over and we're just waiting on a flight home. We don't even have fresh clothes! Nothing! Everything was lost and it's all my fault! Look at her over there! She's never going to marry me now!"

I reached out a hand to his shoulder and offered some gentle assurance, "I may not be able to provide champagne, but all is not lost. If you don't mind, just wait here in the atrium until you see my signal. "

As he walked back over to his would-be fiancé, the wheels in my head were spinning. I grabbed my room service captain, Ben and began to formulate a plan. "I know!" Ben said excitedly. He was always ready with a fun idea. "Let's set a place for them in the ballroom and turn on some music, they can dance all alone in there, it will be beautiful." While normally the ballroom was empty at 9 am on a Sunday morning, we had a movie crew in the hotel filming a story about a snake oil type revival preacher who mends his ways. Part of the cast was a large gospel choir that made for an amazing soundtrack. They used the ballroom to rehearse each morning and I must say it was just beautiful to hear their voices echo down the hallways of the hotel. We needed another place, but the hotel was at full capacity and no open areas were available.

"Ben, get a table, 2 chairs, and full linen set up out back under that little tree, I instructed. "You mean the back lot?" "Exactly!" He called me when it was set up. Ben had created the most romantic setting on the green grass, just under the shade of a blossoming pear tree. The table in crisp white linen, an orange juice carafe with champagne flutes, fresh strawberry cups, and napkins folded like birds of paradise. Ben had brought out the boom box that the banquet staff used to play their favorite jams during room turnovers and ran an extension cord behind the bushes. A little mood music was in order.

Ben, in his white tuxedo shirt and bow tie, tray in hand with a lovely lit candle, and I approached the forlorn man and his significant other, still grieving in the atrium lobby. "Your adventure awaits, sir." I smiled as I prompted them to follow us. Ben bowed.

The gentleman arose and offered his girlfriend his hand. As they followed, Ben and I just grinned. I could see the glimmer of hope and excitement on the gentleman's face as he followed us in faith that something good was in store outside the building. I could even see a curious smile creeping up on his girlfriend.

Ben escorted them to their table, letting them know that while alcohol may not be available till late afternoon, anything on the menu was complimentary and we hoped they enjoy their special setting.

Ben walked back to me just inside the doorway, where we stood for a moment to bask in our "romance mission" accomplishment. Then suddenly, we looked to our left and saw the gospel choir, standing in formation, actually facing the small table! During our set up, people, of course, would walk past us to go in and out of the hotel, but somehow we had missed seeing an *entire* choir!

In a quick moment of panic, I thought, Oh My! How do I ask them to move? I'm sure they came outside because it's a beautiful morning, but would they be willing to go back inside and offer this couple some privacy? I couldn't bear to think of moving this poor couple. But this movie cast booking was huge for business and I certainly don't want to upset them either.

Then before I could speak, in one enormous voice, the choir burst out in unison, "Are you ready for a miracle?" and began singing! I looked over to the little table by the tree, and there was Mr. Forlorn with the biggest smile on his face, quickly dropping to one knee in a marriage proposal! She was elated and the look on her face was priceless.

The music swelled to one of the most upbeat songs I'd ever heard, or maybe it was the moment. Everyone began swinging back and forth and clapping. It could not have been written into a script any more perfect than what was taking place spontaneously in this moment in time.

I saw the couple briefly before their departure and they

seemed a far cry from the mood that encircled them when we first met. The gentleman couldn't thank us enough for providing the most perfect setting for his proposal, and one they would never forget. Did I tell him the choir was an absolute coincidence? Of course not. I believe in divine intervention.

It was about two years or so before that movie came out and I no longer worked for the hotel. While the movie was a definite hit and held great performances by some prominent actors, it was the choir that held a special place in my heart, and that one particular song they sang on that sunny Sunday morning.

The old tattered VHS movie tape is somewhere among my treasured keepsakes because every now and again, I need a good reminding that sometimes when I feel most lost and left behind, the best moments are right around the corner. That asking for help, even from a stranger can bring about good things. And that when you follow in faith, miracles can happen.

The Bible reminds us, "I am the Lord, the God of all mankind. Is anything too hard for me?" Jeremiah 32:27

Sometimes a bad day, a bad week, or a bad experience can make us feel as if our situation is hopeless. We can drown ourselves so much in our misery and frustration, we forget that we may be standing on the edge of opportunity. Dread one moment, utter joy the next. Everything can change in a matter of minutes and often does. It's all in how we look at it.

Are you ready for a miracle?

REFLECTION JOURNAL: ARE YOU READY FOR A MIRACLE?

Think of a time that just when you thought things were at their worst, it suddenly changed. A time when your fears and anxiety were up or on overload and then all of a sudden came in a big swoosh of relief and it wasn't so bad after all. That once frightening nightmare turned out to have a happy ending after all.

Describe it here:

What caused it to change the most? A person interceding?
A new way of thinking? Did something prompt you to look
at it differently? Events went a different direction?

When you become anxious or fearful, what do you do to
try to calm things down? Ask for God's presence? Recite
scripture promises? Deep breathe?

When have you openly asked for help with something
when you felt overwhelmed? Did you receive the help you
needed?

Do you find people are more often willing to help when asked, or not, and why do you think that is?

How can a person's willingness to be helpful be a way to bring others to Christ?

Humans are social creatures. There is a reason that solitary confinement has been used as a form of torture for thousands of years. We need human connection.

Helping each other fulfills the Golden Rule and sets an example of love, trust, and dependability. Accepting help means to be vulnerable, and realize we cannot do everything alone, no matter how strong we might feel we are.

It just might lift someone higher up the mountain to hear how deep in the valley you once were.

THERE IS A MESSAGE IN THE STORY OF YOUR FINDING HOPE.

LEAVING WELL ENOUGH ALONE

It was an awful year. I had been diagnosed with some heart issues that made it necessary for me to see a cardiologist for a complete work up every 12 weeks. My heart was enlarged, and I had three valve leaks. The regurgitating blood would cause me to cough and wheeze and I felt exhausted most of the time. My left leg would swell dramatically and I had numerous side effects as medications were being started and changed and started again. With the complexity of my symptoms, my doctor suggested a full body MRI. When the results came in, he promptly referred me to a surgeon.

"You have three tumors at the base of your brain near the sinus cavity. One appears to be surrounding the pituitary gland. Loss of that gland can mean lifelong hormone replacement and complications, it is also just under the Optic nerve, so there is a 50/50 chance with removal, you may lose your vision. I'd like to operate as soon as possible. Do you have all your affairs in order?"

"Affairs?" I gasped. "Yeah, you know, a medical directive, specific instructions, that sort of thing?" He rambled on as if this was a normal conversation. I guess for him it was pretty routine, but for me, it was a shock to my system. I stared blankly into space. "I'm only 34", I said, "haven't really thought about that." "Well, now's a good time. Let me know what day works best for you and let's not waste any time."

He patted me on the shoulder and left me alone in the room. I remember leaving his office in a daze.

My children were gone for summer break and it was a good thing as I found myself crying often uncontrollably. 3 tumors? Lose my sight? Did I hear all he was saying or only the scary parts? I remember getting into my truck with a very minimal bag of packed items one night and driving aimlessly. I had no idea where I was headed. Just away. Away from the world. Away from everything.

Music was my only companion on that long drive across Texas. I don't recall ever reading a highway sign, just drove endlessly until I dead ended on a beach. I drove out onto the sand a few feet from the water's edge, which I know now to be quite dangerous.

I noticed a post that read North Padre Island. I was

on a beach section of a nature preserve. Great. No people. Just me and mother nature. I stumbled from my truck, tears streaming and walked straight out into the ocean.

I had never seen the ocean other than looking down from a plane before that day, yet I was walking out into it as if it were a long lost friend. Hoping it would wrap me in its crashing waves and ease my sorrows. I went out as far as I could still touching bottom and felt the heavy push of the current sway me back and forth.

I cried out to God. No, that's not accurate. I cried AT God. I yelled at God. I screamed at Him. For all the wasted time. For all the emptiness. For all the hopelessness that still lingered in me with the little hurting child that I had forgotten to console. Where were you God when she was being molested? Where were you God in all the abuse? In all the empty search for love and fulfillment? And now it may be over? Just like that? What is the purpose of this life that has had no purpose? I just got started making things better for my daughters, why am I being thrown this curve ball now?

A wave came in that swayed me off my feet and pulled me out farther from shore. I was suddenly drifting and couldn't find the bottom and as I paddled back inward the sea just pulled me back out again. I stopped paddling and chose to just float and look at the sky. Massive in its expanse, as was this immeasurable ocean. Here am I, but an ant, cursing at my Creator! I wanted the sea to carry me away from all my sorrow and struggles. I contemplated how easy it would be to let myself sink, but as I floated farther out, the more fearful I became. The ocean was so vast. For the first time, I felt incredibly small and insignificant.

Deciding I would not make very good fish fodder, I began swimming back to shore. I walked the beach and found some shells, a few bird feathers, and some interesting pieces of driftwood. A crane or perhaps an egret landed by my truck. As tall as the hood he stood proudly surveying his dinner potential. A beautiful sight in nature undisturbed. I wondered if he ever felt any emotional crisis, understood his purpose, or even cared about the grand scheme of things.

I found myself for a moment relaxing in the sound of the waves, the wind and the occasional gull. Then my self-pity turned into a plan of action. I realized, if it truly was my time to go, then I had much to do. So many things I had been hoarding from God. You know, those sins that you never take to Him because you know that if *you* were God, well, those sins are *unforgivable.* These are the ones in which you knew better and chose them anyway or the ones that you fear somehow fit the description of the unpardonable sin in the Bible.

It was time I laid all things bare. I dug three graves in the sand. Literally, I dug, and grumbled, and cried, and cussed, until I had three reasonably large holes. I figuratively placed my sin and shame into these cold, wet pits. It was a visual experience for me because I need to experience things, see them, touch them, feel them. I then covered them up with sand and shaped the mounds with their own headstones made from my beach collectibles; the feathers, sticks, and shells.

There I sat, just me and my 3 graves, and my endless tears asking God to forgive me and walk me through whatever was to come. I sat there lost in prayer and contemplation losing track of all time until I noticed my feet getting wet as the tide had come in with the sun setting.

I looked down and saw the three mounds had completely washed away! All the work I had put into these little monuments, and in a few moments, they were erased as if they had never been there. I didn't recognize that message. Not yet. I sadly compared their demise to my perceived life and how fleeting it truly is.

I got into my truck, fortunately before the tide moved in any closer, and headed toward the exit road. Reaching for the dial, a random radio station came on with a song I had not heard before that night. I am a lover of words and always draw in to hear what the lyrics have to say. I found myself pulling the truck over in disbelief and letting the miraculously timed lyrics sink in.

"The mistakes I've made, that caused pain, I could have done without. All my selfish thoughts, all my pride, the things I hide, You have forgot about. They're all behind you, they'll never find you,

they're on the ocean floor. Your sins are forgotten, They're on the bottom of the ocean floor.

My misdeeds, all my greed, all the things that haunt me now, They're not a pretty sight to see, but they're wiped away, by a mighty, mighty wave, A mighty, mighty wave. They're all behind you, they'll never find you, they're on the ocean floor. Your sins are forgotten, they're on the bottom of the ocean floor, Your sins are erased, and they are no more, They're out on the ocean floor." (Audio Adrenaline)

I headed home with more assurance in my spirit than a honeybee in a wildflower field and it only took a 10-hour drive one way to find it! Once again, God used music to reach me when I needed it most. I got it! Loud and clear! I was now ready to face whatever may come.

My brother and father drove in from out of state to offer support but a threat from another family member in the throws of a centuries long hatred had them abruptly leaving as soon as I came out of surgery. They didn't want the added stress of family feuding to interfere with my healing. A considerate gesture, but my heart was breaking all the same that this was even an issue. My soul ached that my family could not share the same town together, let alone a room space during someone's crisis moment. I would learn through much prayer that there was a bigger healing needed, and it wasn't that of my surgery recovery, it was my family.

Due to swelling from the surgery, I couldn't sit upright and struggled with eating and taking medication. I was on bed rest for the first couple of weeks. In all the time I spent having a pity party for myself, I didn't make a plan for my children while I was recovering. Their meals, their transport to school, anything. I was so used to being alone that I didn't plan on being in a situation where I couldn't just take care of everything.

I remember looking up to a tray of hot breakfast and a nurse offering my medicines. Then I saw familiar faces with food and prayers, and reports of how the children were doing. As I went in and out of sleep and pain, my precious friend, Jana, a nurse by trade and by heart, had set up and managed an entire schedule of caring for me and my children while I recovered from surgery. Her organized volunteer efforts had covered everything, even laundry, from morning till night, until I was strong enough to care for myself.

It felt like forever waiting for the biopsy report and when the call came, I answered with great anticipation. "I need you to come in, so we can discuss the results," was all that was relayed by phone. I went to the surgeon's office mustering all the bravery I could find. The doctor came in and set his paperwork down. He wheeled his stool closer to me and said: "I have 2 words for you." He then made a dramatic pause. "No Cancer!" I felt the butterflies leave and was overcome with relief.

"I made the decision to leave the one that is around the pituitary until we knew the biopsy results and I'm glad we did. That one posed the greatest surgical risk. *Sometimes you just need to leave well enough alone.*"

That awful year had some of the most amazing lessons for me. I learned that we are never too young to have our "things in order"

That even during the most serious of times, broken people can make things all about them.

That true friends can show up with a plan to carry you when you don't even realize how bad you need one.

Most importantly, my life is a but a vapor, and it is not for me to decide its purpose. God has a plan bigger than my imagination can comprehend. Like that ocean.

And what He has forgiven, is gone. "...as far as the east is from the west, so far has He removed our transgressions from us." Psalms 103:12 (NIV).

Thank God, I am not God. He has forgiven me. I do not have to dig the sins up again when I question whether I deserve what is happening to me. I am His, because of His grace and mercy and when I repented, He washed them away. Yes, the first time.

I need only to see the tide to be reminded my sins have been washed away by a mighty, mighty wave and it is now well with my soul. That is well enough for me, and I agree, when it comes to digging up old sin, we should remember God's promises and like the doctor said, leave well enough alone.

REFLECTION JOURNAL: LEAVING WELL ENOUGH ALONE

Have you ever received an announcement that made you question everything? Perhaps a health diagnosis, a terminal illness, a loved one's diagnosis or passing?

Whatever the situation may have been, the news was so shocking that you had to take a step back from everything and try to gather your thoughts.

What was the news you received? How did you feel about it?

How difficult was it to accept? Did you find yourself in shock, numb? Did you start acting out in anger, disbelief, confusion? What was your reaction?

Did this news cause you to change direction, shift priorities, reevaluate some things in your life? If so, how and what?

Did you ever feel forced to make a choice you didn't want to make? What was it?

Do you feel God was present at this time? Why or why not?

What did you learn from this experience? Was anything gained? Was anything shed or released that needed to be? Anything mended?

Do you believe God can move in big ways when we find ourselves facing huge changes or decisions? How?

Have you ever found yourself in such an emotional state that you completely surrendered to God in prayer? Physically shaken, uncontrollable crying, or something similar? How did you feel?

How did you feel after or what have you learned from that experience?

Have you ever shared that story with anyone? Why or why not?

THERE IS A MESSAGE IN THE STORY OF YOU MAKING IT THROUGH A DIFFICULT TIME.

A PURPOSEFUL CRIME

I was leading a small group at church for singles. We were focused on a study of understanding when we hear God's word. How do we really know that what we are hearing is from God and not just some subconscious murmuring, guilt ridden suggestion, or wild idea? How does one *really* know? My objective was to pray fervently every day that God would show me the answer to this and that I would have my eyes, ears, and heart wide open to receive the message.

It's amazing how foolish we can be in how it is we expect the answer to prayer to come. As if some book would show up or some great epiphany would just enter my head, I waited for the answer to arrive. Little did I know that God was about to work something unexplainable in my life that would go beyond just me and my own situation.

I was leaving my driveway for a potluck at church one night when I felt a very stern pull that I should remove my work equipment from my car. I know it's not wise to leave a computer and projector in your vehicle, but I had a newer car with an anti-theft system and very dark tinted windows. I had kept my equipment in it except for during severe weather for years now, so why change?

I continued to pull out of my drive but now the voice in my head was getting louder. "Put your things in the garage!" it urged. Being lazy, I tried ignoring it but found myself now less than a block away turning around to empty the car of my equipment just to hush the nagging in my head.

I arrived at church and headed to my usual parking space in front of the side entryway. It was dark outside and I heard yet another nagging say, "Park under the streetlight" I heard myself argue in my mind, "Why would I do that? I've parked in the same place for the last 4 years. People will expect to see my car here to know I'm attending." I stuffed the voice in my head down as much as possible and parked in my trusty spot.

Wanting to carry as little as possible, I shoved my small purse and wallet under my seat, grabbed my casserole and exited the car. I made sure to hear the familiar "beep beep" of the alarm system kick in and locked the doors. I stared back at my car as I always did. You see, I loved this olive-green SUV. I loved it more than anyone should ever love a material thing. It fit me perfectly from the feel of the seats to the length in the floorboard to its sporty fun personality. I felt closely attached. Too attached. As I looked back, there was that voice again, this time telling me to not leave my wallet. "I'm at church, for goodness sake!" I smirked it off. What a nagging state my mind was in, I felt I needed to lay off of the caffeine or something.

I didn't stay very long, possibly 20 to 30 minutes at most. For some reason I just remember not feeling right, so after numerous greetings and best wishes, I headed back to the parking lot. I had to stop and squint, close and reopen my eyes, even shake my head, because there in the spot I had parked my car was just an empty space.

For a moment everything seemed surreal. How can a 2000 pound locked vehicle, just disappear? It must be a cruel joke. Someone from inside must have taken my keys and moved it. But wait, my keys were fastened on my belt loop. I never once laid them down!

I searched all around the church and demanded whoever was responsible for this awful joke to confess. I did not have insurance for theft. My daughter had just needed surgery so I temporarily dropped my insurance down to liability to help with the bills. This was not funny.

The police arrived and explained Nissans were hot items and get parted out quickly. The officer stated that if not recovered in the next 24 hours, in all likelihood, I would never see my vehicle again.

I began sobbing uncontrollably. It wasn't because I loved that car beyond all others, or that I had no insurance, no money for another vehicle or even a rental, though these were all good reasons. I cried because I felt like a little girl caught red handed by my daddy disobeying what he had told me to do. I knew immediately that every time I argued with the thoughts He planted in my head, I was disobedient. If it were my own thought, idea, or desire, I would have simply done it, I would not have argued. But because I was lazy, it would have taken effort, or I was concerned with what others might think, I argued and chose to ignore not one, not two, but three sperate messages telling me to protect my interests that night.

Friends kept trying to console me. "There, there, we'll figure out something about getting a car for you." "That's not it, that's not it!" was all I could mumble through my blubbering sobs. That's not it at all.

The police asked for a list of everything that was in the vehicle at the time it was stolen. A leather jacket, a toolbox full of new tools, a Christian CD in the player, my wallet purse, my Bible, my daughter's Bible, and my last copy of the Passion of the Christ DVD. I had bought several copies to give as gifts and had one left that I was unsure to whom it should go and had been asking God to bring that up, so it stayed in my car waiting for that moment.

My friend Jana loaned me her van for work while I tried to comprise a plan for another car. It had been several days.

My SUV was nowhere to be found. Meanwhile, my daughter kept asking if the police had called yet, and did they find her Bible. "I really need that Bible, Mom, it was a special one." "I know honey, God will provide," I'd tell her, and so we prayed that God would bring her Bible back, while in my mind all the while I took note that I would need to swing by the bookstore the next day and get her a new one. Wow, that's some kind of faith, isn't it? Speaking out of the side of my mouth and plotting my own solutions.

The next day I received a call from a detective working my case. They said that a local florist's van was stolen and they recovered it abandoned on the side of the road. In this van, along with all the floral equipment, was my daughter's Bible. I gasped because clearly, God was showing off here. The detective told me that sometimes car thieves will leave articles with other identifying information such as names and addresses to confuse the trail of law enforcement. That detective had no idea the lesson that God was laying before me, so I just nodded and kept repeating "thank you".

My daughter Laci was beyond ecstatic when we went to pick up her treasured book. "Do you see that Mama? Do you see it? We asked Him and He brought it right back! You need to ask for your Bible too, Mama!"

I thought of that Bible of mine. It's one that is so worn the cover fell off, and my mother made a cardboard spine and crochet cover for it. Not worn because I'm such a great Christian, nope, I am anything but that. Worn because of all the crying and clinging I had done to it when it was all I had. Every chicken scratching note I had scribbled in its edges when God showed me one of His promises. It was a treasure to me and my heart sank in thinking it was lost forever. Well, at least her Bible was returned, and yes that was a miracle. How can I possibly ask for more? I will be happy in this little miracle and just keep pushing forward to find a way out of our needing a car dilemma.

A few days later I received a call from the church. I was asked to come down and look at something they needed help with. Luckily, I still had use of my friend's car so I drove down curious to see what it might be. The church treasurer asked me to take a walk outside where he showed me a row of vehicles. Tears filled his eyes as he explained that when news spread of a single mom needing a car, donations came pouring in from out of nowhere. There were cars to borrow for as long as I needed them, cars donated with clear titles to keep, older cars, newer cars, it was unbelievable!

The elders of the church had narrowed down what they felt would be the best choices for me as my job teaching required a lot of travel. I gratefully accepted a Ford Taurus. I was so shaken up by this generosity I struggled to find any word of thanks as acceptable. Words became harder to find as tears of gratitude just brimmed from my eyes. To say the least it was a bit overwhelming.

It had been a couple of weeks when the detective called again. He had quite the story to share. Apparently, there was an entire ring of car thieves operating and after a high-speed chase they recovered a stolen Cadillac on the highway, with, you'll find this hard to believe, my Bible in it. The detective explained again, how common it is for thieves to put a decoy object that has a name on it in a car to throw off the police. I dropped the phone and headed straight to the police station.

You can explain crime theories to me until you are blue in the face, but you don't know my heart experience, my thoughts, my doubts, my shame. Nope. But you recovering my Bible, Mr. Officer, speaks volumes of truth to me. I spent the night in total surrender to God, repenting of my lack in trusting Him. My inward scoffs and lone planning, asking His help and yet pushing Him aside. I cried until that cardboard Bible cover was limp with my tears, truly sorry for my lack of faith.

It had been close to a month now, and no news of my stolen car. The odds of finding it now are a million to one or greater, the detective said. I was teaching in a bad neighborhood at a high-risk school when I started hearing that familiar nagging voice in my head. The one I usually argue with. Only this time, I immediately caught myself as I started to internally reply. It told me I needed to go and look for my car today, myself. For a moment, I thought, "That's like looking for a needle in a haystack! A metro area of close to 200 thousand people, miles away from where it was taken, a month later..." but then I found the strength to shut up and say, "Okay Lord, show me."

I saw vividly in my mind the intersection of two streets, Amarillo Blvd and Martin Road, and then I saw a street sign that read "Dale" I saw it as clear as day. I kept feeling that the second the bell rings I can't waste any time. I needed to get there as fast as I could.

The bell struck 3 o'clock and I flew down to the parking lot and headed east down Amarillo Blvd. Looking left, right, all around me. 'I'm listening, Lord" I kept saying as I found myself at the intersection just as I had seen in my mind. I turned left and the first crossing street was coming up at the corner of a convenience store, and the sign read, "Dale St." and right before me, pulling out of that convenience store, was my car!!!!!!

The hair stood up on the back of my neck! I called 911 and told them I found my car! They asked how I knew it was mine. Well, the roll bars and side steps had been removed from the SUV and the plates were changed to disguise it from being identified, but what they left behind was hilarious. I had various Christian bumper stickers and they were all removed. But I also had an abstinence sticker that I bought at a Lakita Garth conference, and it stated boldly: "No Ringy, No Dingy" emphasizing no sex before marriage. Of all the stickers that had been removed, they proudly left this one on the bumper! I had to chuckle and wonder if the thieves even knew what it really meant.

The dispatcher told me that I should follow while she summoned officers to arrive but after a few blocks, the thieves became suspicious and began speeding. We were driving over 60mph in residential areas when the dispatcher finally told me to pull off and wait at a mutual location. Within 15 minutes or so, an officer came to meet me.

I was jumping up and down and shouting "My car! We found my car!" I was so excited the policeman must have thought me insane. "Now calm down, we didn't catch them, they drove that SUV on terrain we couldn't get to by car, the sheriff is on it now. They will probably ditch it soon." None of that mattered to me. I didn't care if I ever saw the car again, frankly, I saw something greater than I could ever explain! The visual map in my head was REAL, every street, literally placed me directly behind my stolen car! What are the odds of *THAT?*

Later that evening I was called to come and identify my Xterra. It was utterly damaged and hard driven, abandoned in an old overgrown car wash just outside of town. It reeked of marijuana. The police had me go through its contents. There was an infant seat and diaper bag in the back seat, and one baby shoe on the floorboard. Thinking of this family broke my heart. My Christian CD was replaced by an eerie vulgar gangster rap mix. Funny, the items that could have been sold for easy cash such as my leather jacket and tool box were still inside. The only things beside the CD and my wallet that were missing was the copy of the Passion DVD, and of course, the Bibles. The officer said they probably just ditched anything "Christian" after using the Bibles as decoys. After this wild ride, I trust that even a copy of the

Passion that may have landed on the side of a street somewhere is going to end up in the hands God has intended!

You'd think the story ends here, but this just marks a beginning. You see, the church called again. Apparently, an anonymous donor gave 3000.00 and with that and the car and my totaled vehicle, they wanted to purchase a newer better vehicle for me. The elders helped with that too.

This experience was beyond comprehension for me and as much as I wanted to shout to the rooftops what all God had shown me once I finally listened, I found myself unable to speak.

I felt as if I had been hit by an 18 wheeler, utterly exhausted. My nerves were raw. Every moment that I would think of how amazing God is, and how little I am, how odds mean nothing when all is in God's favor, I was left speechless and blubbering. I cried often inconsolably. It took a few weeks before I would recover from this state. Then, of course, I couldn't stop talking about it to anyone who would listen.

I know the story is long, but I had to share it all because of how God used so many pieces to finish the puzzle for me. A couple of years went by and I was at work doing surveys with some temporary help when a woman asked where I went to church. "Amarillo South", I told her. She lit up and said, "Oh my! I know that place!! You'll never believe what

God did for my mom there! She needed a car to get her medical treatment and some lady had just had her car stolen and all these people had donated cars. They gave one to my mom! It was incredible, so many people were helped, she was just one of them!"

I learned numerous people were blessed by the generosity of those who stepped up to donate vehicles. New tires, exchanged engines, you name it. And I was able to finish out that study in our singles group about knowing when God is telling you something in a way I would never have imagined.

I listen now for when I start to argue. When I start to say, 'what about this, and what if they that', I've learned to say, "Ok, Lord, let's do this! Please show me."

"Call to me and I will answer you and tell you great and unsearchable things you do not know." Jeremiah 33:3 (NIV)

"I will instruct you and teach you the way in which you should go; I will counsel you with my loving eye on you." Psalm 32:8 (NIV)

How do we know when God is sending the message? Listen.

REFLECTION JOURNAL: A PURPOSEFUL CRIME

Have you ever wondered if you could actually hear God or know when a prompting direction is coming from Him and not your own thinking? How do you think you can tell?

Have you ever felt God was telling you something but you ignored it? If so, what?

Have you ever felt guilt or shame in not doing something

that you later realized God was specifically directing you to do?

If so, how have you used that experience to be more attentive now and in the future?

Have you repented and forgiven yourself for not being obedient?

Can you look back at any particular circumstance and see the specific good that came out of it? What was it?

Do you think God may allow some trials in our lives to strengthen our character and provide important life lessons?

THERE IS A MESSAGE IN THE STORY OF YOUR OBEDIENCE.

LOVE AND OTHER CULTURAL DIFFERENCES

A friend called me one night and asked if I would be her designated driver. Her plan was to become numbingly intoxicated and I was the last person she could think to call. She was going with or without me. How could I refuse?

Her month had started with her estranged husband dying in an unforeseen accident. She had recently left the relationship which many would describe as abusive and he had always threatened that if she left it would be her fault if anything happened to him. His threats of suicide and aggressive outbursts had become frequent enough that she couldn't take it anymore.

I was told that in a drunken state, he knocked a loaded

shotgun off of the gun rack and that it discharged a shell into his stomach. He passed out and bled to death before any help could arrive. A very tragic and unfortunate accident.

At the funeral, my friend found herself being blamed by various family members for the actions that led to his passing. She just wanted to become numb for a while but had the clarity of mind to ask for a driver.

We went to a local nightspot with very cheap drink specials. I ordered a Coke and she began drinking one of many adult beverages when we noticed two men dancing. Well, not so much dancing, as they were performing. They were facing us. Side by side, arms crossed and doing that Russian kick dance. It was hilarious. Even funnier, was that there was no one else in the club at the time, just the two of us and the two of them. Their dancing really required some kind of bagpipe music, I imagined, yet here they were almost puppet-like to the tune of Oops, I Did It Again. The song ended and they gave a dramatic bow. I noticed how much they looked like the Mario Brothers and couldn't help but applaud their fun little routine.

Soon they were headed to our table. They asked us to dance with heavy foreign accents and I couldn't tell if that was part of the act or not. I obliged but my friend refused and stayed behind. As I was dancing with Khalid, I kept a watchful eye on my friend at the table.

"Why is she so sad?" Khalid asked. "We saw this and tried to cheer her up with our dancing." "Me too," I said as I explained her situation. Some things must just be felt.

They were from the Middle East. Refugees here whose family escaped the Iraqi army with the help of a Christian underground organization.

We exchanged numbers and began getting to know each other by phone the next few days. Having a foreign mother, I have always been intrigued with other cultures and Khalid was never short on sharing stories of his adventures in coming to America or what life was like back in his war-torn country.

He struggled to find steady work, improve his English and help support his mother and sister. They were on public assistance through the refugee program, but what little money Khalid had, he was always free in offering it to help others. In fact, he was so free that as we became closer it began to bother me that due to his generosity he could never get ahead.

His family didn't have a car and walked to the grocery store and so I offered to take them weekly. Each week, Khalid would get the family groceries, and on the way out, there was a bum that always hung around the store. Khalid would give him some various food items and reach into his pocket handing over what little change he had after shopping. "You're not helping him, you know. There are panhandlers like him everywhere, you're just enabling him to be lazy." Khalid would just look at me with his eyebrows raised in confusion. "I don't know what that means. I just give to God." He said.

One day we were stopped at the light of an intersection where a punk-rock looking teenager stood in a leather jacket with a leather choke collar and sporting a spiked mohawk. He held a sign and had his hand out for donations. Khalid asked me to pull closer as he gave his last 3 dollars to him. Frustrated as we drove away, I argued that if this guy really needed the money he could pawn his jacket and that he would probably just go and buy drugs or alcohol with what we gave him.

Khalid looked at me very seriously and calmly said, "Who am I to say what he does? Perhaps my dollar is the one that buys the alcohol that takes him to the bottom and at the bottom he realizes, wow, that man who didn't know me gave me his last dollar! Maybe that bottom is where he finds God. I don't give my money to him, I give it to God. What that man does with it is not my business."

I drove home in silence at the profound insight I just heard and felt ashamed of the many times I have talked myself out of helping someone when I originally felt drawn to do so. Even though I am reminded in Mathew 5:42 to **"give to the one who asks you, and do not turn away from the one who wants to borrow from you."**

I went to meet his mother and sister and they were the most hospitable people I have ever met. I was given a warm welcome and offered a delicious middle eastern dish of dahlma which soon became my favorite. I commented on how beautiful his mother's necklace was and she immediately removed it and gave it to me. I kept telling her I could not accept it, but she insisted I take it. "You must!" She said.

At another dinner, when I commented on her new shoes, she insisted I take them too,. After much fuss and my not accepting her shoes, which were half my size by the way, I appeared to have wounded her deeply. Khalid later told me that his family believed when someone likes something of yours it is considered envious. To honor God, you are to immediately give it that item to them, he explained. They felt this kept the curse of envy away and showed a sacrifice of not coveting material things, After learning that, I had to reign in my usual compliments whenever I saw them.

Khalid came over to visit me one morning and asked, "How is your neighbor on the right?" I said, "Fine, I suppose." He then asked about the one on the left. I said I didn't see them much and didn't really know. "And the one across the street? How is their health? Do they need food? Do they have everything they need?" I explained how that most of that was really none of my business and that even though I had lived in my home for close to 5 years I really didn't know much about any of them.

He seemed shocked. "You mean you don't check on your neighbors?" I looked at him blankly, "No that's not really my responsibility." "Then whose is it?" he replied persistently. "Everyday, you are to check on your neighbors and help each other! What if he needs help and no one checks? I don't understand this country." He shook his head.

Wow. After hearing it like that, neither do I.

How often do we quote the Golden rule? **"And as you wish that others would do to you, do so to them?"** Luke 6:31, and **"For the whole law is fulfilled in one word: You shall love your neighbor as yourself."** I had given those verses a lot of lip service, but Khalid brought them to life in the way he lived.

Khalid learned a lot about Jesus from the Christian ministry organization that helped his family flee, and he often wanted to pray, but he would always ask me to say the actual prayer. He said he loved Jesus but since the commandment said to not put any other gods before God himself, he asked me if I ever wondered if I offended God by praying in Jesus name. No matter how I explained the relationship, Khalid would always come back to, "I just don't want to offend Him, I mean the prayer from my heart, just you say the 'in Jesus name' part if we have to say that." I never explained to Khalid's understanding that believing in the Son did not offend the Father. The concept of the Holy Trinity was sadly lost in my translation.

Khalid would bring me flowers from the roadside and even pebbles that would come with elaborate stories. He would describe how a certain stone that was shaped like the moon reminded him of my face smiling. A flower's petals resembled tears that he said love would wipe away. A true romantic and storyteller was he. I could listen to him for hours. Though he earned a pittance in whatever odd job he could get, the special dates we went on together were simply magical.

When a good song came on the radio, Khalid would insist we park the car and dance. Time with him was thrilling. He was invigorating and full of life. At first, I thought this came from escaping the life he lived before coming to America, but now I am convinced it was because of it.

There is a sensitivity and an awareness that comes only when we know our days are short and everything can be lost in the blink of an eye or the drop of a missile. It comes from seeing suffering, true suffering, and knowing that the only way to eradicate it is with the preemptive strike of love. It is to check in and check on others and share everything you have been blessed with, big or small. It is to live presently, eyes open, in every moment.

There is a love that becomes palpable when we set the example like Khalid. "Do not neglect to do good and to share what we have, for such sacrifices are pleasing to God." Hebrews 13:16.

Better still, it comes with a promise. "Give and it will be given to you. A good measure, pressed down, shaken together and running over, will be poured into your lap. For with the measure you use, it will be measured unto you" Luke 6:38

REFLECTION JOURNAL: LOVE & OTHER CULTURAL DIFFERENCES

I've always thought of love as an action more than a feeling. Dr. Maya Angelou is famous for quoting the expression that "people will not always remember what you say, but they will always remember how you made them feel."

Try to recall the last Random Act of Kindness you committed. What was it?

Do you feel it made a difference?

What do you wish you would do more often for others, but time, work, and other obligations tend to get in the way?

What would make it easier for you to do this?

What kind of support system do you have? Family? Friends? Neighbors? Church family?

Do you check on each other? Actively pray for each other?

Are there ways in which you could support each other better? If so, how?

If someone has helped you by praying for you, checking on you, bringing you food, helping you monetarily when they can, or with other basic needs, how did it make you feel?

How did it feel the times you have helped others?

THERE IS A MESSAGE IN YOUR STORY OF LOVING THY NEIGHBOR.

SINGING FULL CIRCLE

When I was a pre-schooler in Missouri, my mother worked in the housekeeping department of a nursing home. She hadn't lived in the U.S. for very long and was excited to be promoted to Housekeeping Supervisor, even with her broken English. My parents were recently divorced, and my mother worked hard to make ends meet for me and my two brothers. Affording a babysitter was not in the family budget, so I spent many days with her at the nursing home. While she worked I was charged with two very important tasks: staying out of sight and keeping quiet.

I still remember the sights, sounds, and smells of the home. There was a lobby area where staff would bring out residents to sit together each day. I was perplexed at how sad they looked to me. Many of them wheelchair-bound, with their heads pointing to the floor. No one talking. The occasional cry out for help. I started creeping my way into the lobby to get a better look and noticed that when they saw me, more often than not, they would smile.

I knew then, this was the place I was supposed to be. Not being the shy one, I decided to grace them with a musical performance. My repertoire consisted of about two songs at that time. Somewhere Over the Rainbow and Jesus Loves Me. I would sing them repeatedly. Yet, no matter if it was the first time or the tenth time, my song was always followed by smiles and pats and applause. The room seemed to light up and what had seemed so terribly sad seemed happy for a moment.

I couldn't wait to go to work with my mother as I felt I was going to work too. I had a mission. It broke my heart on the days I wasn't allowed to tag along, but eventually, I started kindergarten and my visits were fewer and fewer. Then my mother remarried and we moved to Texas.

Music always remained a big part of my heart. I was in the band in middle and high school and volunteered in church and community choirs. I sang a few times with different groups and praise teams and was part of a choir that released a CD that raised money for charity.

I would DJ any party. I would offer singing telegrams for friends, and when karaoke became a "thing" it became my number one hobby. Anyone who has ever really known me knows how important music is to me.

I moved back to Missouri in my forties and started a career in home care. Part of my job was being sent to make personal client visits. A good part of customer service was visiting our clients when they had the unfortunate event of a hospital admission or required the level of care only received in a nursing home or rehabilitation facility. Naturally, a song was one of the first things I pulled out of my bag of tricks during a visit where it seemed someone could use a bit of cheering up.

Sometimes the visits were friendly and sweet. The client and their family would be pleasantly surprised to have a visitor. Others were bittersweet. I remember many of them who had no family near and my visit was the only one they would receive. I'd bring the company's standard "goody bag", crossword puzzles and reading materials, and let them know when they came home our staff would still be there and ready to help them.

Yet still, some visits were heart-wrenching. A frightening diagnosis, an uncertain outcome, the news that someone will never go home, the sadness of family nearby but no one is visiting, a dark room, a quiet, depressing air. It felt somewhat awkward walking in with a big smile and saying "I brought you a goody bag!" to someone in such despair.

I would touch their hand and let them know I was there and that I could just listen if they wanted to talk. I could pray if they'd like, or just sit too. If they wanted me to stay all they had to do was squeeze my hand or give me a sign. During the times I had no idea what to say to offer comfort, but the person was so desperately squeezing my hand, a song would usually come to mind.

Sure, I would sing just about anything they asked me to if I knew it, church hymns, Frank Sinatra, old country classics, you name it, but sometimes a specific song would come to mind and with their permission, I would sing it to them.

When the song was over, we would just sit in the quiet. Sometimes a tear or a deep breath would come, and the client or another family member present in the room would mention it was exactly what was needed. I left in awe, rewarded that I was able to serve someone in a difficult time just by being there with a song.

Soon my position evolved to include taking my karaoke machine to different nursing facilities across the region where I would set up in a lobby or dining area and residents would join along singing. The power of music is indescribable. It is a medicine of the heart I do believe. We would clap as we sang, evoking wonderful memories of days gone by. I have to say, it was one of the most rewarding parts of my career to see this kind of happiness, yet it certainly was never in the job description.

One day, I was singing in the lobby of St Luke's Nursing Home. There was a piano in the room that seemed oddly familiar, but then again, many of these facilities have very similar settings. Someone requested I sing Somewhere Over the Rainbow. As I sang, I was transported back in time. There I was, a little girl of maybe 5, in a blue sailor suit dress, big blue bow in my golden hair, beaming proudly as I belted out Judy Garland's song from Wizard of Oz. I later asked a staff member if this was the only lobby area and she described to me how the building had been remodeled but if she recalled correctly, the piano I remembered used to be in this very spot.

Here I stood, where I stood as a child, almost forty years later, singing the same song. It wasn't planned that way at all. In fact, I had only moved back to Missouri in the last couple of years at that time. The territory was too unfamiliar to me to even know where I was without the help of GPS, yet I believe God brought me full circle with a song for a reason.

He showed me that music of the heart isn't about being on a stage, having a bunch of fans, or being admired, it's not even about being able to sing well. It's about making a difference in another's life, in just the right moment. I know how much God has spoken to me through music and to be a part of it reaching someone else is the most wonderful feeling to me.

You have some sort of a gift, a talent, a hobby. A way of sharing happiness, starting a conversation, spreading a little joy. If you really think about it, it's probably been a part of your life or at least an interest for many years. Have you ever considered sharing it?

Gifts were made for giving. The Bible tells us, "Each of you should use whatever gift you have received to serve others, as faithful stewards of God's grace in its various forms. 1 Peter 4:10-11.

The connections and rewards that come back in return are some of the most beautiful life has to offer.

REFLECTION JOURNAL: SINGING FULL CIRCLE

Sometimes we rediscover an old talent or desire that we put on the shelf for far too long becomes center stage once again and can now bring us much happiness and bless others as well.

I have a friend who ended up marrying her high school sweetheart, 30 years later after a "chance" meeting brought them back together again. They hadn't seen each other in all of those years and now share a very beautiful life together.

When have you noticed God using something or someone from your past to make a difference in your present?

Is there a hobby, or skill in your past that held so much joy for you that you now miss it? What stops you from bringing it back?

Have you ever been somewhere and felt a flood of memories or thoughts that brought you to a sweet recollection or time of gratitude?

Do you feel coming full circle happens by chance or is there something more meaningful to it? Write your thoughts here.

THERE IS A MESSAGE IN YOUR STORY OF SWEET SURPRISES.

BRINGING LIFE TO DEAD PLACES

Recently I went with a colleague to a local nursing home to assist her with providing an activity for the residents there. We were making sun-catchers. A simple piece of plastic produced in various shapes, such as hearts, crosses, and butterflies. Once painted and hung in a window, these would shine a colorful light into someone's room as the sun's rays beam through it.

Our group of participants consisted of an elderly woman wheeled to the table, her head bowed to her chest and snoring, a middle-aged veteran who suffered a severe head injury during an active duty conflict, a gentleman struggling with severe pain and unable to walk, but hopeful for a new pair of shoes, and a quiet little lady who came in on her own accord, sitting down and getting right to work to paint a flower.

I was assisting the veteran, who had chosen a vivid blue, to paint his sun-catcher, "All blue," he said, for the heart that he selected. Due to brain damage from his injury, I am assuming, he would repeatedly introduce himself, thrusting out a hand for shaking and offering a very well-mannered "What is your name?" We could trail off into conversation momentarily, but inevitably the introduction would return. After restating my name, he would say, "Well, Mica, I love you a million billion 24 trillion." To which I would smile and thank him kindly. He never tired in his approach, always cheerful and inviting. Despite repeating himself, his genuine disposition in offering a warm welcome and great love was quite delightful.

Some time passed and I moved over to assist the older gentlemen, perhaps in his seventies, in the wheelchair, and asked how he was doing. He told me that he hasn't been able to walk in a while and that he was told he just can't anymore. He said he lost the feeling in his legs and battles a lot of pain, but he was just certain if his son brought him a new pair of shoes that he could walk again. I asked when it was he saw his son last, and he said he couldn't remember but he waits for those shoes every day because he is sure once he puts them on things will be different.

Each time my colleague walked over and he found himself between the two of us, he would smile and begin to chuckle. I said, "You sure are happy today despite hurting so badly." He just beamed and replied, "Well, look at these beautiful women all around me!" With a gleam in his eye, this elderly man looked up at my co-worker and said with a sly grin, "I'm only 50, you know!"

Lastly, I joined the quiet one as she was finishing her craft. She turned to me and asked me if this was what I do, bring activities to people in nursing facilities. I told her that I was blessed to do it occasionally but as my responsibilities have changed, I wasn't able to visit as often anymore. There was a time when I would go into these places and sing to the residents. They would sing with me and I must admit, I've had some of the most magical moments of my life doing that. But life gets busy, and I found myself cutting that out entirely.

She could sense my melancholy and grabbed my arm. Looking straight into my eyes, she very firmly said, "Sing to me!" We had talked about the difficulties of life for just a bit before and so I sang to her a song by Kathy Troccoli, titled "How would I know?" about how the hardest trials in life can make us thankful. Then we just sat there a moment, both tearful, holding hands and taking a very deep and conscious breath.

She turned her frail frame toward me as if to demand attention and I have heard her words echo within me for days now since. "When you share your gift, you bring life into a dead place. Coming here, sharing a craft, singing a song, sharing your time. It brings life into a dead place. Don't you EVER stop doing that!"

I understood her description all too well. That "dead place", meant so much more than any physical place. It was a place of the heart I felt she was describing, where burdened souls have given up and begin to merely exist versus truly live. It's not just a problem in some elderly, losing hope. That dead place could be a metaphor for some of our homes, our marriages, and workplaces too.

The scripture, **"Therefore encourage one another and build each other up, just as in fact you are doing."** (1 Thessalonians 5:11) reminds me that we are all going through something no matter our stage of life, and it is a great help to support one another.

We helped hang the little masterpieces in the residents' rooms before saying our goodbyes and I couldn't help but think how blessed I was that day. In a little over an hour, I received some valuable life lessons.

Sometimes you just need a nap. It doesn't matter what may be going on around you, if you need to seize the opportunity to get some rest, then do it.

Never miss the chance to reach your hand out and introduce yourself, you just might make a new friend.

Never grow tired of telling someone you love them or get tired of hearing it. An expression of love is a priceless thing and some of us need to be reminded we are loved, repeatedly, and unashamedly. Even a million billion twenty four trillion times!

Hold on to your hope, whether it is in the Calvary coming or the Fountain of Youth, we all need to believe in the positive, for it is our faith that keeps us going.

Never get so busy that you stop sharing. Your time, your talents, your ear, your shoulder. Like the sun-catcher, beams of warmth can radiate through you to others in the simplest deed. There is a place in which you can be a light, do not enter it blindly, go in blazing, I say. It will indeed bring life to a dead place.

REFLECTION JOURNAL: BRINGING LIFE TO DEAD PLACES

While this story talks about sharing your time and talents to bring happiness to others, hopefully with the previous chapters, you have begun reflecting on that in your journal entries.

Meeting new people is such a precious opportunity to explore the diversity that is humankind. Every detailed and unique personality that presents itself before us holds its own opinions, wisdom, and adventures.

Some folks become hardened and weathered souls, dead to

life and love. Yet some beam brightly an enlightenment for anyone near them.

How do you feel others see you?

What was the last story someone shared with you that left an impression?

How did it make you feel? How would you describe the connection? Sad, humorous, informative? Something else?

What was the last story that inspired you spiritually or encouraged you to take some sort of action?

Why do you think the person shared this story with you?

Think of a great storyteller you know. What makes their stories so interesting?

Do you notice any kind of theme in their stories? If so, what? Life lessons, a funny punchline, a moral to the story?

Has anyone ever told you they appreciated a story you told them, or that it helped them? Perhaps they told you that you should write a book?

These can all be cues that your message made a serious impact.

THERE IS A MESSAGE IN THE STORY OF DISCOVERING YOUR GIFTS.

CREATING LOVE

My mother grew up in Germany in the 1940s. A time and place after the war that most of us would not envy, but it taught her a resourcefulness that surpasses any I've seen. You see, my mother was re-purpose before re-purpose was cool.

Let me explain. Every kitchen rug we had, she had made herself, by stripping old sheets and shirts and braiding the strips together. When she wanted new throw pillows, retired socks and old recycled nightclothes made for great stuffing. She had an eye for re-coloring, re-building, and reinforcing anything that she tired of or simply desired to have for us.

Pantyhose were a big thing in the 70s and 80s, women never left home without them. Only they didn't last very long. Despite nail polish and hairspray attempts at saving them, one good sized run and they were ready for the trash.

Not at my house. The legs became straps and ties, stuffing, and straining and holding gadgets for numerous purposes.

My mom was unstoppable when it came to pantyhose. In fact, I don't remember ever owning a curtain rod. She would hang the nails, thread a hose leg through the curtain and tighten up the end. No one was the wiser. They made great elastic for the waist of your outgrown pants too!

When my bedroom was getting boring and I wanted new wallpaper, my mother took my stack of Tiger Beat, Teen Bag, and Star magazines and covered my walls with Farrah Fawcett, Leif Garrett, Shawn Cassidy, and any other hot celebrity of the day! With star-studded wallpaper, I was the envy of my adolescent friends.

I remember as a child, my favorite time of year was returning to school after Christmas break. The time when your friends gathered together and compared stories of what presents they received for Christmas. Now if you know my family, you might think that odd, because this single mother of mine, with her thick German accent, was working hard to feed three children, and she didn't make much.

We lived on "Commodity foods." That was a welfare type program where families who qualified, meaning the dirt poor, could pick up sugar, flour, macaroni, and powdered milk in bulk, among a few other things, for free, to help put dinner on the table. Some of my favorite meals involved those ingredients, like sugar noodles and milk toast. Funny. I find myself craving them still today.

It's amazing the ideas you can come up with when you are forced to use what you have. We may have been short on money, but my mother was never short on ideas. She could make something out of nothing, and that something was really, well, something to see.

At Christmas, we always had so many gifts. If you're the kind of kid that counts and compares, that means a lot. "I got 5 presents! How many did you get?" Someone would inevitably ask. Should I be honest and tell them 12 or would that be bragging? How did I have 12 presents when my mother scrambled to make ends meet? Let me tell you, she knew how to shop!

My mother was and is the Thrift Store Queen of Every Good Deal. Instead of pouring that hard-earned ten dollar bill into one cheap new toy, she would hunt and scour every thrift store to find thoughtful gently used gifts that were exactly what I wanted.

It never occurred to me that my toys didn't come wrapped in plastic or have new tags attached. All I saw was that I was literally surrounded by gifts! Gifts, gifts, and more gifts. There were items that we would never have been able to afford and yet some family was disinterested enough to donate it, and now it was mine to treasure!

I can see myself now, sitting by the tree, buried in piles

of wrapping paper (that consisted of newspaper and grocery bags carefully cut to wrap my presents). I'm telling you, she was resourceful. She would look at us beaming while we unwrapped. Our joy was her reward for her hard work.

When anyone asked where I got my new doll or record player, or whatever the object of adoration may be, I proudly said, "My mother got it for me!" I felt sorry for my friend who received 1 pair of Gloria Vanderbilt jeans when I was given 3! A turquoise pair, a royal blue pair, and a maroon pair! So what, if mine came from the thrift store? No one knew!

It wasn't even the number of gifts that was the big deal, really. It was the thought and creativity that went behind each and every little thing about a holiday or special occasion that my mother orchestrated.

There were games. There were adventures. There were treasure hunts.

She was a creator and inventor of surprises.

I owned my own Post Office when I was in 3rd grade. How many children can say that? Yep, I certainly did! It was a giant box, probably an old appliance box, that my mother transformed into a working post office. Fully decorated on the outside down to its title and address, I could step right up and put a coin in the slot, and out would come a roll of stamps from behind the scenes.

My mother would wait patiently behind the box, while I put another coin in the slot for an envelope and then she would slide it out to the front counter. To me, it was the very machine at the Post Office and I was learning a life skill, ta boot!

My favorite gift was a dollhouse. My mother found the perfect dollhouse for me but it had no furnishings whatsoever. So, every night for weeks, she toiled to fill the house with what she felt it would need to welcome its new family.

She created a TV set by using a cardboard matchbox and gluing a movie scene she had cut out of a TV guide onto the front. She drew channel knobs, and there it was! She made a bed from a carefully reconstructed pudding box and it even had cloth blankets and pillows that she had sewn by hand.

Quite the interior decorator, she had made miniature rugs and curtains to match the bedroom set! There were cabinets and even lamps and accessories crafted out of everyday items. Pictures hung on the wall of beach scenes she had clipped from a magazine and framed with matchsticks.

It was extraordinary.

Down to every detail.

I don't think there was any way I could have truly

appreciated these acts of loving service as a child, for what they truly were. I was too excited to just get busy and do what kids do, play. I know now that the time it took to think of, collect, construct, and design that house and that Post Office down to every miniature detail was an amazing act of love. It didn't cost her money. It cost her time.

Another way she shared her time was getting on the floor and playing with me. From feeding the postal machine to playing house, to putting on puppet shows with adorable characters that yes, she constructed from thrift store items and old socks. My children have been fortunate enough to have experienced her puppet shows, and as the torch is passed, my daughter now grown, built a puppet set with my grandsons and they performed an act with their own precious creations for a holiday not too long ago.

When I think of all the money spent on the latest toys that are played with but a moment and the next moment the child has moved on, I appreciate the thrift stores and our ability to not only recycle but to donate and shop for meaningful causes. Knowing my items and ultimately, money, is going to help the disabled, the Veteran's, the blind and numerous other causes feels good. I'm quite proud to play a part in their existence.

However, the true spirit of resourcefulness, recycling, and re-purposing that I admire most, I must credit to my mother, who showed me with a little bit of creativity and a lot of love, the best gifts are right in front of you.

One year, I saw a television show that took a tour of Elvis's mansion and fell in love with animal print. At that day and age, animal print was mainly for pajamas only and material was either hard to come by or highly expensive. That didn't stop my mother in her quest for surprising me and bringing home a new little adventure! She found every zebra, giraffe, tiger, or leopard print nightgown, robe, or house slipper in every thrift store in town. A dollar here, fifty cents there, and we had an interior designer's treasure chest full!

After some detailed trimming, we had enough material to cover 3 lamp shades, 2 large picture frames, 4 gorgeous throw pillows, make a window scarf, and even cut out a fake tiger skin throw for the coffee table. Guests would often ask who helped me decorate and where could they get these items. The transformation to my living room was amazing!

They say everyone has a different love language. Some people express their love by saying it, others in giving gifts, spending time, or performing an act of service. Other share a hug, a pat on the back or hold a hand. Sometimes wrapped up in our own language, we can miss what is being expressed to us.

There is a quote, I am unsure by whom, that states, "A child spells love, T-I-M-E" Looking back now, at the effort my mother took in the gifts she gave, I realize how much she loved me. No money could ever buy the memories she gave me. That was the time when being poor brought about some of my richest years.

Times grew difficult for us as I began to get older, and the relationship between my mother and I became distant and conflicted. Over the years when things were the most challenging, I would find myself remembering those times when she showed me how to make the most of things, no matter how little you have.

I believe the resourcefulness and creativity my mother taught me carried me through when my daughters were growing up and we struggled to make it. Looking back, I believe it gives me an appreciation for all things.

I have lived in times of need and times of plenty, never knowing when a sudden change was right around the corner, and believe me, there have been a few sudden changes!

Proverbs 27:23-24 says, "Look after your sheep and cattle as carefully as you can because wealth is not permanent. Not even nations last forever."

Learning to manage what you have and be content builds a strong, resilient and thankful character.

REFLECTION JOURNAL: CREATING LOVE

Have you ever had a lack of something and had to "make do" with whatever resources were available? Think about that for a moment. Write it down.

What is a way you have expressed your love to someone that did not cost any money?

In what ways did a parent or primary caregiver show love to

you? With words? Actions? Hugs and snuggles? Material things? Or just spending time with you?

How do you feel these actions may have affected your view of God and His relationship with you?

Sometimes, we do not receive love in ways that we are able to recognize it or receive it, and sometimes people are in a place or condition in where they are simply unable to express love.

I spent many years of my adult life carrying wounds from my childhood that I internalized into not feeling loved or even feeling worthy of love. Only by God's grace and wisdom has He shown me that what I was feeling was only the reflection of another's actions, and ultimately wasn't about me. My clinging to that hurt, though, was molding my path into an unfavorable one.

By coming to accept what was and forgive all of the should-haves and could-haves of my childhood, I became able to look back and find these beautiful moments when love was in fact expressed and that there were many good things that came out of my upbringing.

I can celebrate those now. And I can see so very many messages in my childhood story. Signs and people, events, and what can only be credited to the divine maneuvering of my life's puzzle pieces. Good and bad, they have all culminated to who I have become, to my crying out to God and to my recognizing His gentle knock on my heart's door.

How has your childhood shaped you as an adult? Are those ways positive or negative?

What from your childhood needs to be accepted and forgiven in order for you to find any messages God has for you?

THERE IS A MESSAGE IN YOUR STORIES OF FINDING FORGIVENESS AND EXPERIENCING LOVE.

WHAT'S THE MESSAGE IN YOUR STORY?

I was watching a tree while waiting in a drive through line for a taco. Yes, just a simple tree. It was the beginning of Fall, and the leaves were just making their way to the ground. Some of them. Some still held on for dear life. It was a mix of greens and golds and oranges. Beautiful. And I couldn't help but think of this tree, this life, and the predicament it was in.

You see, no matter what storm comes, a tree is stuck there. Rooted deep. It has no option to pull itself up and move to a better site. Surely it did not choose to be stuck in a 12-inch path aligning a curb along an asphalt drive-thru, yet here it is in all its glory.

I could relate to this tree, finding myself in life and health situations I did not ask to be placed in.

I wondered if the tree ever thought, "It is what it is." or if it knew of the scripture stating about after having done all else, to just stand. (Ephesians 6:13). I've heard that if man never praised his Creator, even the stones would cry out. (Luke 19:40), and that "the mountains and hills shall break out in song and the trees of the field shall clap their hands." (Isaiah 55:12).

Can you imagine, being stuck in circumstances beyond your control, and still praising?

The drive thru was backed up and I was actually grateful, just sitting, pondering. I imagine in the Spring, this tree was full of life, squirrels and birds making homes, and surrounded by the annual flowers strategically planted around it. Now as the winter steadily approaches it will soon stand bare and alone. I thought of the seasons in nature and how they parallel our lives. Spring, full of promise and new beginnings, birth, creation, and the height of beauty. For us, this must be birth to age 25.

Then approaches Summer, a time of fullness and basking in the sun, as when we meet the achievements of family and career. This must be 25-50. So busy had I been then accomplishing all I felt was expected, was deserved, was normal, that before I knew it, here came Fall.

I turned 50 this year. A time of slowing down, and cooling

off, a time of preparation for winter. A letting go of what is now dead and dying. I prefer to use the word "transition". This Fall phase would be age 50-75.

Lastly comes Winter, when everything silently falls asleep. A time of bitter cold and yet a beautiful blanket of white that cleans away the old, and feeds the younger life with itself as it slowly leaves. I sat there staring at this tree and felt we could truly relate in those things.

I too, still have green leaves. Dating, learning new things, like creating a blog, writing a book, and life after my children have moved out and married. Life as a grandmother. Exciting new parts of who I am.

"There is a time for everything, and a season for every activity under the heavens..." King Solomon declares in Ecclesiastes 3:18.

Every season of our lives has its stories. These are the day-to-day exchanges, events, and experiences that shape us and I believe God has messages written in those experiences. Messages just for us. Messages meant to be shared. Messages that, no matter how simple or crazy or miraculous they sound, have the power to forever change and save lives.

I am absorbing every nugget of wisdom I can glean, yes, even from a tree, that helps me explore my thoughts, my existence, and this amazing gift we call life.

We must strive to be mindful of asking God for His wisdom in recognizing the message He has for us. Messages in our past and those yet to arrive.

If we keep our eyes, hearts, and minds open, there is so much to be learned along the way. But don't keep all that great insight to yourself! Call up a friend and go for coffee. Or just be mindful during a conversation, even with a stranger, when you can personally relate to what they are expressing, sharing what God has shown you in a similar situation.

By sharing the stories of what our Heavenly Father has done in your life, we are spreading the message of the Gospel as an authentic representative. The message that our Savior is ALIVE and CARES about our circumstances. That He reaches out to us and longs to be known in so many wondrous ways and to know Him is to be FORGIVEN and set FREE.

What are you waiting for? There is someone waiting to hear your story.

What's the Message in YOUR Story?

INVITATION TO SHARE YOUR MESSAGE

Encouragement is more than a passing compliment, smile, or pat on the back. While these can certainly brighten someone's day, deep down we may hunger for something more filling. A kind of encouragement that strengthens us and lightens our load by knowing that our burden is shared.

Sharing your personal stories is one of the most meaningful and heartfelt ways to share the love of Christ.

For inspiring messages of what God has done and is doing in people's lives Go to **The Message in the Story** on Facebook. I invite you to submit your story or testimony there to be shared to encourage others. It may also be considered for inclusion in a future edition of The Message in The Story.

Be part of a movement in encouraging our brothers and sisters in Christ to share their messages and stories. Your message can be another's turning point.

I'm grateful for you taking the time to read this and I pray it blesses you as you reflect on the many messages God has for you.

To God be the Glory.

References

All scripture references in the book are from the **New International Version** of the Holy Bible, unless otherwise noted. The author uses the **YouVersion mobile app of the Holy Bible** for daily scriptural references and studies. The app offers multiple Bible translations. NIV was chosen by the author simply for reader clarity within the topic context.

In **Love and Other Cultural Differences** the main character name used is fictional to preserve the actual person's anonymity, while the story itself, as well as all other stories and characters involved are non-fiction, true accounts of events as recalled by the author.

Ocean Floor by **Audio Adrenaline,** from the album **Lift,** released 2001, produced by **Audio Adrenaline** on **ForeFront** label. Lyrics can be found at https://www.metrolyrics.com/oceanfloor

A Baby's Prayer, Help Me God, and **How Would I Know** by **Kathy Troccoli,** are on the album **Love and Mercy,** which was released in April 1997 and produced by **Peter Bunetta,** on **Jive Records.**

Amarillo South is a nondenominational church in Amarillo, Texas, now a campus of **Hillside Christian Church**, located at 6901 Bell St, Amarillo, TX 79109

ABOUT THE AUTHOR

Mica Burnett is a mother, grandmother, pet mama, and poetry lover. She enjoys nature and finds inspiration in even the most ordinary things.

She has been publicly speaking for over 20 years in areas of education, healthcare, community awareness, and personality and relationship enhancement.

Passionate about sharing inspiring stories and the reason for her joy, she has often been told she should write a book to expand her reach. After a few long talks with her Heavenly Father, and waking from a dream with a full chapter list, The Message in The Story is her first complete published book in this effort. She also authors a blog entitled Hope, Health and Heartfelt on WordPress.

Her poem **Forgiving My Unforgivable**, A personal journal of healing from abortion is available on Amazon.

Mica is available for conference and community speaking across Missouri, Kansas, Oklahoma and Arkansas. To get in contact, please visit **www.MicaBurnett.com**.

* 9 7 8 1 5 1 3 6 3 7 3 0 3 *